MASTER TODAY'S MOST POPULAR VIDEO GAMES!

16 bits of gaming entertainment were cool. 24 were even better. But with Nintendo®'s new 64 bit gaming system, video games are taken to a whole new level of quality—and playing will never be the same. With sharper graphics, more realistic sound, and more challenges than ever, you need to know the amazing secrets only a master video game guide could provide. **HOW TO WIN AT NINTENDO® 64 GAMES** gives you the hot inside tips, cheats, and codes that will make you a pro, in front of the video screen—and beyond!

HOW TO WIN AT NINTENDO® 64 GAMES

HANK SCHLESINGER

St. Martin's Paperbacks

How to Win at Nintendo® 64 Games is an unoffical guide, not endorsed by Nintendo®.

Nintendo® is a registered trademark of Nintendo of America, Inc.

HOW TO WIN AT NINTENDO® 64 GAMES

Copyright © 1999 by Hank Schlesinger.

ISBN: 0-312-97087-0

Printed in the United States of America

St. Martin's Paperbacks edition/August 1999

10   9   8   7   6   5   4

To Melissa Suzanne

ACKNOWLEDGMENTS

I'd like to take this opportunity to thank my two intrepid game and code testers, Vincent "Vinny" LaFace and Matthew "Matty Boy" LaFace. I couldn't have done it without you guys.

CONTENTS

CONTENTS

AIR AND WATER RACING

ADVENTURE RPG, PUZZLES, AND OTHER GAMES

ADVENTURE AND ROLE PLAYING

PUZZLES AND OTHER GAMES

ACTION

FIGHTING

COMBAT GAMES

INTRODUCTION

So, you want to play like a pro? Do you want to kick butt? Do you want to send your opponents screaming in agonized defeat from the room? Do you want the glory? The legions of fans? How about the fame and fortune? Do you think you can handle it? Do you have what it takes?

Unfortunately, there is no fame, no fortune, no legions of fans. And most opponents over the age of six won't go screaming from the room. So, calm down, okay? Good.

The first thing you should know is reading this book won't make you a better player. Only playing a game can make you a better player. That's true for baseball, football, basketball, chess, and, yes, even video games. The more you play, the better you get. This has been true since ancient times when humankind was living in caves and playing Pong by firelight. It was true when your parents played Pac-Man or Space Invaders. (Note: A good test is to get your mom or dad to play Pac-Man or Space

Invaders. If they're any good at all, then you know they wasted a lot—a lot!—of time pumping quarters into machines.) Only playing makes you better. That was true then and it's just as true today. It's a fact of life. So deal with it. Reading a book, even this informative and excellently written book, will not automatically make you a better player. The only thing that will make you a better player is playing the games. However, there have been some changes over the years.

What has changed, of course, are the games. There wasn't much to learn about Pong or Space Invaders. Knock the blip to your opponent's side of the screen or blast the invaders. It was all fairly simple stuff, which is why your parents probably aren't very good at today's video games. Many of the games for the Nintendo 64 system are incredibly complex. You could play these games for hours and hours on end until your hands swell up to the size of toilets and your eyeballs bulge hideously out of your head. That's just about how long it would take to learn all the tricks and strategies.

Or you could simply read this book. Take my word for it, hands the size of toilets that are permanently bent to hold a video game controller and bulging eyeballs are not considered attractive. They will not prove to be an advantage at any point in your life, unless your main goal in life is to scare small children and animals. So let's get started with a few basic phrases.

Cheats:

From the time you were little you've been told it was wrong to cheat, right? Cheating was bad. Only cheaters cheat, right? Okay, one of the coolest things about video games is that *cheating is allowed*. Not only is it allowed, but manufacturers encourage it. They want you to cheat. In fact, they build the cheats right into the games.

A cheat is a secret code built into a video game. A cheat can be practically anything, from extra or unlimited lives to additional weapons or secret powers for your character. Often these codes can be punched in with the controller at the beginning of a game when the menu comes up. Sometimes the cheat codes are entered during the game. Codes can be anything, from entering a secret password to executing a series of special moves during game play. Finding out when cheat codes can be entered is one reason for reading this delightful and entertaining book.

Legend has it that hundreds of thousands of years ago, game designers put cheat codes into games to make testing them easier. Programmers would use the codes for their own testing, but it was only a matter of time before players discovered the secret codes and began swapping them. Video game cheat codes became more and more important as time went on. In fact, cheat codes became so prized among players that game manufacturers took note and began including them in the games as a playing feature. Today discovering the codes and mastering them are as much a part of the game as winning.

Easter Eggs:

You don't hear much about these in video games anymore, mostly because they're called *tricks*. A trick, like a cheat code, is a secret program designers insert into the game. Tricks began as a game designers' way of playing a joke. They have nothing to do with helping you win the game, they are just funny things designers put in to make themselves and their friends laugh. And again, like cheats, players soon discovered them and game manufacturers began putting them into games as a player feature. Like cheats, tricks or Easter Eggs can be activated by everything from a secret password to a series of special moves while playing the game.

Secret Characters, Hidden Characters, and Just Plain Weird Characters:

I have to be honest with you, I don't know how this started. Game designers are a wild and crazy bunch. But the best games include a bunch of *secret characters* or *hidden characters*. Sometimes you fight them in a bonus mode, and other times you need to enter a password or code to get to them. Sometimes these hidden or secret characters have special powers that can help you win a game, but other times they just have weird body parts, like huge, giant heads or feet. Go figure, right?

Secret Modes:

More often than not, *secret modes* have nothing to do with winning the game. Just like the secret characters, you get to these modes by entering a password or code. Sometimes you get an entirely new type of game, but other times you get to play the original game in a weird place.

A large part of this book is about cheats, secret modes, and secret characters. Frankly, they just make games more fun to play.

A Short Dictionary for the Video Game Player

AI: Short for *artificial intelligence*. When you play against the central processing unit and it seems as if you are playing a real person, that is an AI function. Of course, it really isn't "intelligent"; the CPU is simply following programmed instructions that go something like "If the player does that, then I do this . . ." A more accurate description would be "fake intelligence." If the system were really intelligent, it would be able to do your homework, take tests for you, and answer really tough questions, such as why charcoal isn't really made out of coal.

CHEAT: A feature concealed in the game by programmers to make the game more enjoyable or as a reward for playing the game well. Also, a hidden option in a game that gives you an advantage.

CART: Video game slang for game cartridge. The small square unit that houses the game and plugs into the console.

CODE: A password or buttoning sequence that opens special options in a video game. Just like a cheat, codes can be placed in a game to make it more fun or for use by programmers. Codes can include passwords to new modes or bonus levels. They also can disable or add features in a game. (In this book, U stands for up, D stands for down, L for left, R for right, A for A button, B for B button, and so on.)

CONSOLE: The N64 unit that plugs into your television or VCR is the console.

CONTROL STICK (also called joystick): The directional stick with knob on your controller.

CPU: *C*entral *p*rocessing *u*nit. It is contained in the console and serves as the brains of the game. It is used most often in describing your opponent when in single-player mode.

FAQ: An abbreviation for *f*requently *a*sked *q*uestions. (Get it? FAQ.) However, it is pronounced "Facts." So there is a double meaning there. A FAQ guide can include everything from a few simple codes to a complete walk-through of each level of a game. It also can include problems players may encounter often in game control.

GAME PACK (or GAME PAK): Slang for game cartridge.

JOYSTICK: Big arcade games have a directional control that consists of a golfball-size ball on a stick that fits your hand and controls the direction of play. On your controller you have a *directional pad* and a little joystick or *control stick* just big enough for one digit (finger or thumb).

MODE: How the game or character plays. For example, on a race game you might drive the same track in time attack mode trying to beat a preset time; however, you also might drive on the same track in battle mode where the object is to crash into other players. The mode in which you play a game determines character movements and your objective. While there are some generic or standard modes, such as time attack, other modes have names made up for a particular video game.

OPTIONS: Features in a game that you can choose. This gives you the ability to set the game play to include characters with big heads, for example, and is easily done from the opening screen. *Option* is also the ability to set the game for different types of play: one player, two player, battle mode, and so on. When features are not listed under options and/or require secret codes, they are cheats, tricks, and Easter eggs.

PAD: The directional button on the controller, usually with movement in eight directions. Its operation is like a joystick, without the stick part. It's also called a joypad because it moves like a joystick.

PAK: Slang for cartridge (see **Game Pack**) but also can mean an optional device such as a controller pak that fits onto the game allowing for more features.

PLATFORM: There are two meanings for this term. In a video game, a platform is something that a player jumps on to or jumps from, such as a floating raft on a lake. The word also can be used to describe the type of software system or even the type of console used to play a game. Usually these descriptions are by brand name, such as Nintendo.

PLATFORMER: A video game in which the major action involves the hero jumping from one platform to another.

ROLE-PLAYING GAME
(ALSO CALLED RPG): A game in which the player assumes the part of the game's lead character to explore the multienvironment world of the video game on a quest. These games most often involve solving puzzles or obtaining weapons or special powers in order to complete the quest. In some of these games, the question (or mission) takes place in a single building, such as a castle, with the player exploring the different rooms. In more complex games, the quest takes place in a highly detailed alternate world. And in still others, the game play may move the player from one miniworld to another.

TIME ATTACK: A mode in which you try to beat a set time. You play against the clock rather than an opponent.

SIM: Slang for *sim*ulation. A sim is any game that puts as many realistic details as possible

into the game play. A game that features a realistic cockpit of an airplane would be a sim,
but a few action games and role-playing
games now fall into that category. Sim means
real, the way things work in real life. Basketball players who can slam dunk are sim; players who can fly and walk on other players'
heads are not sim.

WALK-THROUGH (or WALKTHROUGH
or WALK THROUGH): Detailed step-by-step
and screen-by-screen instructions, either written or drawn, that tell you how to beat a
game in CPU as opponent mode.

What Makes a Video Game Fun?

Well, a long, long time ago video games
weren't fun. They had titles like Growing Brus-
sels Sprouts and Clipping Toenails. And only a
few really, really weird kids played them. Big
problem. So, the guys who made the games de-
cided to make them fun. This proved to be a
major breakthrough for the business. One of the
important things they discovered is that the act
of learning makes the games fun. Learning how
to get through tricky parts or finding out all of
the secret stuff is a big part of what adds to the
fun of video games. Naturally, the more you
play, the better you get at the game. You begin
to win. This is true when you are playing

against the computer or against friends. And winning, of course, is fun. So, the more you win, the more you play, right? Well, almost.

If the game is too easy, nobody wants to play it. A game that's too easy is almost as bad as a game that's too difficult. It's boring. Learning how to play the game is half the fun. The other half is winning. Together, winning and learning create what's called a learning curve. Draw a half circle on a piece of paper with the round side up. That's the curve. You start at the bottom of one side playing the game and learning all you can. That moves you up the side of the curve. Once you reach the top of the curve, learning all you can or want, the game becomes less fun and you begin to play it less and less. That's the downward side of the curve, It's the opposite of riding a bike up a hill. The fun part is not going up the hill but going down it. That's why even your favorite game gets boring after a while. And that's why the manufacturers started putting codes and cheats into games, to give you more to learn. Codes and cheats, along with extra modes and levels, keep the game from becoming boring too quickly. Yes, learning is fun, so you could also call a learning curve a fun curve. That's just the way your brain works.

Hey, What's This Book About?

.So, by now you're probably asking: What's in this book, anyway? And why am I reading all this stupid stuff? Are *all* the *secret codes, cheats, tricks,* and *strategies* in this thing? The answer is no. Hey, I have to be honest with you, right? A single video game can fill an entire book with its codes, cheats, tricks, and strategies. What I've done is taken what I feel are the most useful, the most interesting, and the weirdest codes, cheats, and strategies for my favorite games. The sections are arranged by types of games, that is, sports, racing and driving, adventure, and action. There are one or two main games listed at the beginning of each chapter. These are the most popular, the best, or my favorites. These games are explained and described in detail, so that you get an idea of what they are about. After that I've included some of my favorite cheats, codes, and strategies. The main games are followed by other similar games for which I list cheats, codes, or strategies without a lot of detail up front.

Now, I didn't list any walk-throughs, and I'll tell you why. For one thing, I don't believe in them. I think they make the game less fun. It's the difference between exploring and going on a trip with a map. Video games should be *ex-*

plored, not mapped out and planned like a family vacation. The second reason is, and you probably know this, that games are so complex that strategies for a single game can fill an entire book.

You should also know that I didn't review or rate any of the games. I figured, what's the point? Why include bad games in a book to begin with, right? I picked the games that I liked best and put those in the book. Some of the games are better than others. All of them, I think, are pretty good. Video games, like anything else, are a matter of personal taste. Some people like driving games and others like role-playing adventures. No one type of game is better than any other, so I tried to include as many different kinds as I possibly could. I also tried to include a full range of games, from easy to difficult.

If you're just starting out with using cheats and codes, this is as good a place as any to start. With practice, some of them will make you a better player and others will just make you laugh. In my opinion, there's a bunch of people out there who take video games way too seriously when they write about them. Reading about video games should be fun too. The main thing is still to have fun. Remember, they're just video games.

And, as to the second question, "Why am I reading all this stupid stuff?" I have no idea. If I were a kid, I would have turned directly to the actual cheats and codes. So, you better stop reading right now. Immediately! Stop reading before you learn something.

A Note to Parents

Video games are fun. There is no getting around that fact. They are part of a kid's life and one of the many entertainment choices he or she has today. However, as the technology has improved over the years, games have evolved in a fashion similar to movies to include a wide variety of themes, content, and situations. That is to say, not all games are suitable for all age groups. Just as all movies are not suitable for young children because of violent or adult content, the same holds true for video games.

To their credit, the video game manufacturers have acted as responsible adults in the matter. The formation of the Entertainment Software Rating Board (ESRB), supported by the video game industry, independently rates all video games in much the same way as movies are rated. Indeed, as the available technology allows for ever more detailed screen representations, today's games move ever closer to movielike action. For that reason, parents should select video games as cautiously as they select movies.

It is a parent's responsibility—along with the

youngster—to carefully monitor the types of video games that come into the home. Clearly displayed labeling that lists the ratings on packages make this job easier. But it is up to the parent (and kid) to learn the rating symbols and what they mean.

Following is the ESRB's rating system.

- **E is for EVERYONE**. The designation of E indicates that the game has content suitable for ages six or older. Older games (those rated prior to January 1998) may be rated K-A, which is an identical rating.
- **T is for TEEN**. This designation indicates that the game is suitable for kids 13 years and older.
- **M is for MATURE**. This designation indicates the game includes content that should be restricted to people 17 years or older.
- **A is for ADULTS ONLY**. Games with this designation should be played only by grown-ups.
- **RP is for RATING PENDING**. The game has not yet received its final rating from the ESRB.

These ratings and a rating icon should be printed on the lower left- or right-hand corner on the back of the game box. Important information regarding the rating is also listed on the back of the box, describing the type of action and material included in the game. If the box has no explanation on the back, the game does not contain content that might cause concern.

A Bunch of Stuff You Should
Know About This Book

I've done the best job I could in getting the best, most accurate descriptions of games, codes, cheats, and strategies into this book. I tried to write it the way I'd like to read it, with a little bit of humor. But let's face it, things sometimes happen. Some of the jokes in here might not be too funny. Some of the information might not be accurate. If any of the information is wrong, it was not done on purpose. I apologize. My dog ate the computer.

Nintendo Fun Facts
(Bet You Didn't Know Any of This Stuff)

The video game industry makes more than $15 billion worldwide. Over 40 percent of all American households own a Nintendo product. A good way to check this is to go around to all your neighbors and ask. For every ten houses you ask, at least four should own a Nintendo game. I'm just kidding, please don't do that. All your neighbors will think you're really weird.

Eventually your parents will be forced to move to a new town where nobody has ever heard of you.

Nintendo was started in 1889. It was tough going those first couple of years because both TVs and video games hadn't been invented yet. Okay, seriously, the company started out making playing cards. So you see, they've always been into games.

Nintendo made its first home video game system in 1977.

When Nintendo released the N64 system in 1996, more than 500,000 systems were sold the first day. Today there are more than 7 million N64 systems out there. How many games is that? It's a lot. If you took all the N64 systems and placed them end to end, it would mean you have way too much time on your hands.

What Nintendo game contains the most data? The answer is Zelda: The Ocarina of Time. The game contains 256 megabytes of information. Okay, so you probably knew that.

SPORTS

BASKETBALL

GAME NAME: NBA JAM

ESRB RATING: E for Everyone.
Content suitable for those 6 years or older.

THEME: Real professional basketball simulation

PLAYERS: 1 to 4

DEVELOPED BY: Acclaim/Iguana WestMidway

COMMENTS: We're talking five on five here. A big step up from other Jam titles in the past that featured two-on-two action. This is *real* b-ball, the way it was meant to be played! No, I don't mean it's better sitting on the couch than playing basketball. I mean this is real sim. This video game features all 29 NBA teams and a knock-out graphics package.

Because the game is based on a high-tech simulation engine, each NBA team plays like the real NBA team. For instance, you can do the Sonics' trap, the Celtics' press, and the Bulls' triangle offense. The system has also incorporated individual players' styles and signature moves, including free-throw stylings and routines.

The game features five modes: shoot out, with a free throw and three-pointer contests; exhibition, which offers a single-game play; season, which provides a realistic NBA schedule; custom season, which allows you to change the length of the season and schedule; and, of course, playoff, which allows you to forget all the preliminary games and go right to the play-offs.

This game was designed to reward knowledgeable players. This is a fan's game. You have more than 300 players here and a play-calling system that NBA scouts designed specifically for the game. So, to master the game you're going to have to be up on your b-ball stats and knowledge. Players here have their real playing skills and special moves. If you're not up on these, then spend time in the scouting reports mode and gets your facts and stats right. Also, be wary of playing too aggressively. Players can be injured. Worse, these injuries carry over from one game to the next and can screw up your season.

This is b-ball without a lot of the nonsense and horseplay of some of the other games. After all, who likes that kind of stuff, anyway? It's dangerous. You could hurt yourself or something. Maybe even take an eye out.

Game play is critical in this game, and you have to take it seriously. That means realistically. For instance, in other games you can run like a maniac for the basket and the computer won't do anything. Well, no such luck in this game. However, while plugging those holes that made other basketball games unrealistic, the designers also went to the trouble of incorporating a ton of realistic plays into NBA Jam. So what if you can't make 9 billion three-pointers in a row? The computer has a huge library of plays that let you coach like a pro. This is a trade-off that anyone serious about b-ball should be willing to make.

Tip:

This tip won't help you win, but it is pretty good. You can get multiple camera angles while on the free throw line by pressing the R button before you shoot. Will it help your shot? Nope. But, like I said, it's still an interesting feature.

Codes and Cheats:

Change Shooter at the Free Throw Line: If you get to the free throw line with a less than excellent shooter, you can switch the shooter by changing ''Player Match-Up'' under settings.

Long, Long Dunks: To enable the long range dunk mode, pause the game play. Then press Left, Left, C-Down, Left, Left, C-Down, Left,

Left, C-Down, and Z. You'll hear a tone to confirm that you did it right. Now whichever player had the ball can dunk from anyplace on the court, but just until the buzzer sounds at the end of the quarter.

Biggie Players: For large players, pause the game and enter: Left, Left, C-Right, Left, Left, C-Right, Left, Left, C-Right, Z. You will hear a sound to confirm that you entered the code correctly.

Teeny-Tiny Players: For small players, pause the game play and enter: Left, Left, C-Left, Left, Left, C-Left, Left, Left, C-Left, Z. You will hear a sound to confirm that you entered the code correcty.

Easy Shooting: To make the shot every time, pause the game and enter: Left, Left, C-Up, Left, Left, C-Up, Left, Left, C-Up, Z. You will hear a sound to confirm that you entered the code correctly.

THE BEST OF THE REST: BASKETBALL

GAME NAME: **KOBE BRYANT IN NBA COURTSIDE**
ESRB RATING: **E for Everyone. Content suitable for those 6 years or older.**
THEME: **Professional basketball**
PLAYERS: **1 to 4**

DEVELOPED BY: Nintendo

COMMENTS: Very, very realistic and enough weird secret codes to keep you playing even if you aren't a huge basketball fan.

Big Heads: Pause during a game and press Right on the control pad twice. Then press Left on the control pad, the R button, Z button, Start, A button, Start, A button, Start. When you return to the court, the players will be in big-head mode.

Hidden Teams: To access the hidden teams, hold L when selecting Pre-Season lineups at the main menu. You have to search out the hidden teams from the regular ones. Hint: They are named after Nintendo.

Disco Dancing: Start a game and then hit pause. While still paused, enter the following code: A, C-Up, control pad Down, control pad Up, C-Down, R, R, B, C-Right, C-Right, Z. Get ready for the light show! (Note: Don't panic! I know you went into instant replay. That's okay. They designed the code to work that way.)

Tiny Basketball Players: Go to the main menu and enter the following code: C-Right, C-Right, B, R, R, C-Down, Up, Down, C-Up, A, and Z.

Hang on the Rim: After a two-handed dunk, press B and you'll hang there on the rim. Note:

If you insist on hanging up there for more than a few seconds, the ref will call a technical.

GAME NAME: **NBA HANG TIME**

ESRB RATING: **E for Everyone. Content suitable for those 6 years or older.**

THEME: **Professional basketball players and teams**

PLAYERS: **1 to 4**

DEVELOPED BY: **Williams Entertainment**

COMMENTS: There are a ton of codes in this hoopfest. So, even if you're not a hardcore hoops fanatic, you can still enjoy Hang Time. Following are some of my favorites.

Codes:

Go to the Tonight's Match-Up screen. Press the Turbo button to change the first digit, the Shoot/Block button to change the second, and Pass/Steal to change the third. To use more than one code at a time, two players must be on the same team. If two players are on opposite teams, then you can use only one code at a time and both players must input the code.

Action	Code
Block Power	616
Max Power	802

Action	Code
Unlimited Turbo	461
Tiny Players	025
No Pushing	390
Tournament Mode	111
No Music	048
Stealth Turbo	273
Max Speed	284
Legal Goal Tend	937
Quick Hands	709
Hyper Speed	552
Fast Passing	120

Rodman Make-Over: Go to the Select Teams screen and press Up or Down on the control pad to highlight the Chicago Bulls. Dennis Rodman should be shown among the players at the bottom of the screen. (If he isn't, press Left or Right until he appears.) Then press Pass and the statistics for the team and Rodman's hair will change.

Big Head Mode: Go to the Tonight's Match-up screen and press Turbo and Pass together.

Really Big Heads: Go to the Tonight's Match-Up screen and press Up, Up, Pass, Turbo.

Display the Shooting Percentages: Go to the To-night's Match-Up screen and rotate the control stick in a 360-degree circle clockwise. (That's all the way around in a complete circle, starting with Up.) When you complete the circle, hold Up. The Shooting Percentage indicator will appear at the bottom of the screen.

Colorful ABA Ball: Go to the Tonight's Match-Up screen and hold down the right button and then Shoot, Turbo, and Pass.

Random Team CPU Selection: Go to the To-night's Match-Up screen, hold Up, then press Turbo.

Play on the Roof: Go to the Tonight's Match-Up screen, hold Left, and then press Turbo twice.

Max Power: Go to the Tonight's Match-Up screen, press and hold the Shoot button. Then rotate the control stick clockwise until the game starts. Your player will have maximum power.

Big Time Power Options: Go to the Tonight's Match-Up screen, press Up, Right, Down, Left, Start, A, B, Y, X. Your player will have Unlimited Turbo, Hyper Speed, Max Block, Max Speed, and Fast Passing.

Hidden Players: Go to the Enter Name screen from the main menu and into the enter name mode. In this mode, enter the name and the pin number listed by each name to select that player.

STAFF PLAYERS

Name	Pin
Daniel	0604
Morris	6000
Shawn	0123
Root	6000
Nfunk	0101
Amrich	2020
Sno	0103
Eugene	6767
Bardo	6000
Eddie	6213
Mednik	6000
Japple	6660

Duplicate Hidden Players: Select Enter Name from the main menu to access the enter name mode. Then enter the name/name abbreviation and the pin number listed by each name to select that player.

(REAL BASKETBALL PLAYERS)

Name	Pin
Kidd	0000
Glennr	0000
Hgrant	0000
Kemp	0000
Smits	0000
Pippen	0000
Motumb	0000
Webb	0000
Stackh	0000
Malone	0000
Rodman	0000
Ghill	0000
Ewing	0000
Cliffr	0000
Webber	0000
Mursan	0000
Davidr	0000
Starks	0000
Dream	0000

Name	Pin
Johnsn	0000
Rice	0000
Mourng	0000
Ahrdwy	0000
Elliott	0000
Miller	0000

(Note: You probably know who these guys are, so I didn't list their full names. If you don't know who they are, well, they are professional basketball players.)

PROGRAMMER PLAYERS

Name	Pin
JC	0000
Minife	6000
MXV	1014
Danr	0000
Jason	0729
Munday	5432
Jigger	1010
Divita	0201

Name	Pin
Jfer	0503
Marty	1010
Jamie	1000
Patf	2000
Quin	0330
Marius	1005
Turmel	0322
Jonhey	6000
Carlos	1010
Nick	7000
Mortal	0004
Kombat	0004
Perry	3500

(Note: No, I didn't list the full names of these guys, either. They are game programmers and not professional athletes.)

GAME NAME: **FOX SPORTS COLLEGE HOOPS 99**
ESRB RATING: **E for Everyone. Content suitable for those 6 years or older.**
THEME: **College basketball**
PLAYERS: **1 or 2**

DEVELOPED BY: Z-Axis

PUBLISHED BY: Fox Sports Interactive

COMMENTS: A solid game featuring favorite teams from the NCAA. What's the drawback? Well, there aren't any real-life players in the game. NCAA rules won't allow the college hoopsters in video games. In a way, this gives the game a longer life. In a few years you won't be stuck with a bunch of players who are either long forgotten or moved on to the pros. However, you do get authentic heights and weights and 120 top teams. For added realism there are also authentic arenas and team logos. And then there's a host of bonus all-conference teams dating back to the 1970s. Like pro-themed games, you can play an entire season or jump into exhibition or postseason play for shorter rounds or single games.

There's also plenty of playing realism here, with players faking and setting picks. The game also features a Fan Participation button that you can press after making a play to hear announcer Ken Frazier do a commentary. There's also some goofiness in the codes, but not a lot. Depending on how much you like college hoops, the game is either great or a yawn. However, it is fun to try to match the real players to the game's players by their height and weight.

Codes:

To work these codes, go to the Secret Codes screen on the option menu and enter them.

To Get Rid of the Fans in the Arena: NOFANS

To Have Your Players Look Like Ghosts: GHOST

To Play Half Minute Halves (60-Second Game): THIRTY

For Big Head Players: NOGGIN

For Trails on the Ball: TRAILS!

To Play on a Custom Court: Z-WOOD

To Play as the Game Designers: TEAM-Z

To Access Different Announcer Commentary: MONKEY

To Turn Off Shot Clock: BUZZ

To Have More Fouls Called on the Home Team: HOMIE

FOOTBALL

GAME NAME: MADDEN NFL 99

ESRB RATING: E for Everyone. Content suitable for those 6 years or older.

THEME: Realistic professional football

PLAYERS: 1 to 4

DEVELOPED BY: Electronic Arts/Tiburon

COMMENTS: So, you want to play football? If you want to knock helmets with the pros and hear the cheer of the crowds, you can't do much better than Madden NFL 99. The Madden games get better with each edition, and 99 is no exception. There's not as much Madden commentary on the sound chip as some people would like, but the quality of game play more than makes up for it.

Madden 99 is a masterpiece of realistic graphics. I mean, we're talking the kind of graphics that lets you read the team logo on the helmet. Stadiums, too, are realistic. And as long as we're talking realism here, there's plenty of solid, realistic field action. Hey, you don't even have to know how to play the game to have fun with this baby, just go to one-button mode that controls all the action from a single X button. This is a good way to learn, but don't become too used to it or you'll miss all the fun. However, one added benefit of the button is that it allows you to play with someone younger or not as knowledgeable if he or she is the only one around. So you can tear your little sister away from Mister Rogers to play some football.

Now, here's the bad news. The controls are a bit wacky if you're not using the one-button mode. The X button becomes the #1 receiver; the A button is #2; and the B button is #3. Hey, I can't help you with this, you're just going to have to practice. And believe me, it takes a bit of practice. Don't expect to take the game out of the box and play like a pro right away. Give yourself some time to get used to the controls.

The other thing you're going to have to practice is your running game. This title moves a little slower than other football games. There's an advantage to developing a solid running game. Many of the features built into Madden 99 give you a lot of choices when running. For instance, you can dodge around players more easily or break through a tackle without hitting the green stuff. Also, if there's an opponent coming your way, just hit R2 and you'll dodge him nicely.

And here's another tip: Madden 99 might be

a little *too* realistic. Sure, you can hear the helmets hit, but sometimes it's tough to see what's going on. In fact, the replay gives better coverage than the actual play, much like a real game. So, watch carefully. Pay attention to the replay and remember just how the play went down. Believe me, that will help you loads in the future. Make use of that replay button!

Now, a little more bad news. Okay, not real bad news, but there aren't a lot of custom play options in Madden 99 compared to some other games. Most of the time you're playing this game, you'll be playing right out of the team playbook. This is a positive thing if you like realistic games. However, if you like to get a little creative in your video football, then you might be disappointed.

We're talking real football here. So, here's another tip. When you're blitzing the quarterback and he is out of reach and about to pass, hit the jump button. It'll take a little practice, but after a while you'll be able to judge the distance it takes to knock down the passes.

Codes and Tips:

There really aren't a lot of secret codes and stuff here in Madden 99. And that's probably a good thing, if you like realistic football. After all, who wants to be playing a game and have a goofy friend start punching in codes to make your quarterback's helmet turn into a turnip?

And as far as strategy goes, well, you'll be playing mostly from team playbooks, which are very realistic. However, there are a few fun codes, which, thankfully, don't mess up the game play very badly.

Random Stadiums: At the stadium select screen, press R or Z.

Hidden Teams: Enter one of the following codes at the code entry screen:

Team	Code
NFC Pro Bowl	BESTNFC
AFC Pro Bowl	AFCBEST
All-Madden	BOOM
All-Time Stat Leaders	IMTHEMAN
60s Greats	PEACELOVE
70s Greats	BELLBOTTOMS
80s Greats	SPRBWLSHUFL
90s Greats	HEREANDNOW
All-Time Greats	TURKEYLEG
NFL Equipment Team	GEARGUYS
75th Anniversary Team	THROWBACK
1999 Cleveland Browns	WELCOMEBACK

Team	Code
EA Sports	INTHEGAME
Tiburon	HAMMERHEAD

Tomato Quarterback: Enter the code "SPLAT" at the Code screen.

Dancing Ref: Press B, B, A, C-Up at the Coin Toss screen. .

High Stepping Deion: This is actually a pretty cool feature that can be done with *any player you like*, not just Deion. As you score a TD, run toward the end zone, but be sure there is plenty of distance between you and your opponents. Ten yards is fine, but more is better. If you don't have enough space, then it will be really embarrassing. After you pass the five-yard line, press and hold the C-Up. This may take some practice, but with any luck, you'll have a lot of practice scoring touchdowns to get it just right. Anyway, when you do it just right, the player will dance into the end zone.

GAME NAME: NFL BLITZ

ESRB RATING: E for Everyone. Content suitable for those 6 years or older.

THEME: Professional football fun

PLAYERS: 1 to 2

DEVELOPED BY: Midway

COMMENTS: So, maybe you're not a purist when it comes to football. Maybe you like a little goofiness in your game. If that happens to be the case, then NFL Blitz is the football game for you. If you remember the arcade hit, then you remember that it has great graphics, weird options, and realistic play. The same is true for the home version.

There are two playing modes in NFL Blitz: *season mode*, which offers a realistic-type 17-week season that includes playoffs and the Superbowl (though the coolest thing about this mode is that the computer keeps your stats, schedules, and all the rest). Then there's *arcade mode*, which is basically a single game.

Now, in case you didn't know it, here's the news with NFL Blitz: You can create your own plays with the Play Editor. Even better, you can take your Nintendo 64 to the local coin-operated NFL Blitz, whether it's in an arcade, bowling alley, whatever, and plug it in to execute the plays on that unit.

So, without further delay, here're the codes that will have you doing things on the gridiron that no NFL player has ever done.

Strategy Tips:

If you read only one tip in this section, then read this tip. Remember, when playing a two-player game, you must hide your cursor. This will leave your opponent in the dark about your strategy. The code (also listed below) is to go to playbook and press Up twice on the upper left play.

Remember, when playing the computer, stick as much as possible to a running game. And be afraid, be very afraid of the system's passing game. There are a couple of reasons for this. The first one is that the computer will cheat. Sad, but true; the CPU has been programmed to put in unlikely fumbles, interceptions, and missed field goals. The reason for this, or so the designers say, is to make the game more interesting. After all, a computer can't compete with a person. So, to evade these CPU cheats, try to avoid a heavy passing game. This strategy will prevent the heavy fumble and interception game. As much as possible, try getting knocked out of bounds rather than tackled. And remember, if your turbo power is low on a tackle, then you are more prone to fumble.

When the opposing team is about to go for a field goal, move a defensive man to the right side of the formation. With a little practice you can tackle the place kicker. While this is tricky, once you get it down pat, it can be very effective.

If you're about to make a first down or TD but have players closing in on you fast, then jump. You usually can get another yard or so as the defensive man pushes you forward.

An absolute vital move is to remember that

by tapping the turbo button twice you will spin. This is an essential move for avoiding ugly defensive men.

For an on-side kick, hold Up then press Turbo, Jump, and Pass after scoring. A little trick to getting an extra blocker while hiking the ball can be accomplished by holding Turbo, Jump, Pass, Down during the hike itself. You can add a little mystery to the game by hiding the play cursor. This is done by pressing Up twice on the upper left play on the playbook screen.

One of the really cool features in NFL Blitz is the ability to play as a weird player. For instance, you can play as Raiden from Mortal Kombat 4 by entering the name Raiden and the code 3691 on the initials screen. Other trick players, including members of the design team, are as follows: At the Enter Name screen, type in one of the following names/abbreviations and PIN numbers to play as one of these people:

Name	PIN	Hidden Player
Turmell	0322	Mark Turmell
Sal	0201	Sal Divita
Jason	3141	Jason Skiles
Jenifr	3333	Jennifer Hedrick
Daniel	0604	Dan Thompson
Japple	6660	Jeff Johnson
Root	6000	John Root

Name	PIN	Hidden Player
Luis	3333	Luis Mangubat
Mike	3333	Mike Lynch

Cheat Codes:

They say there are two ways to skin a cat. Personally, I don't even want to know the first way. However, this is a perfect opportunity to show that codes can be written in different ways depending on which book, magazine, or web site you're using to cheat. Following are the two most popular ways to write or format codes by gaming enthusiasts.

In Example A, you have to get down and count the number of times you hit Z, B, and/or A then the direction Up, Down, Left, or Right. In Example B, numbers are used to represent the number of times you hit Z, B, and/or A then the direction Up, Down, Left, or Right.

The following are real cheat/trick codes for NFL Blitz, so try them out. Also, I'm feeling extremely mischievous, so the codes in Examples A and B don't match exactly. For instance, to make it rain you perform the exact same actions in both Example A and Example B; they are just written or formatted differently. However, there's no way to make it snow in Example A, but there is in Example B. There is absolutely no reason why making it snow couldn't be shown in both formats, except that the guy supplying the cheat codes either didn't know how to make it snow or wanted to keep it secret so he could amaze his friends. On the other hand, there are instructions on how to get an extra blocker in Example A but not in Example B. This actually has a reason. The extra blocker action doesn't fit into the way Example B was formatted because it is performed during actual play. Now, here's a challenge that will make your parents wonder why in the heck you keep looking at the same pages over and over and doing everything on your Nintendo twice. Because in at least one more instance, I gave the code in one example and not the other. While you're cursing me under your breath, I am throwing my head back wildly and laughing.

EXAMPLE A

Go to the Versus or Match-Up screen and press Turbo (default is Z), Jump (default is B), and Pass (default is A) to change the icons below the helmets. After the icons have been changed, press the D-pad or stick in the indicated direction to enable the code. After a code is entered correctly, you'll hear confirmation from the game. The following are chosen on the Match-Up screen:

No CPU Assistance: Press B, A, A, and Down. Please note that in a two-player game, both players must enter the code.

Show More Field: Press B, B, A, and Right. And again, in two-player mode, both players must enter the code.

Fog On: Press B, B, B, and Down.

Thick Fog On: Press B, B, B, B, A, and Down.

Fast Turbo Running: Press B, B, B, A, A, and Left.

Huge Head: Press B, B, B, B, and Up.

Super Blitzing: Press B, B, B, B, A, A, A, A, A, and Up.

Big Football: Press B, B, B, B, B, and Right.

Hide Receiver Name: Press Z, A, A, and Right.

Tournament Mode: Press Z, B, A, and Down (two-player game only).

No Play Selection: Press Z, B, A, A, A, A, A, and Left. In a two-player game, both players must enter the code.

Super Field Goals: Press Z, B, B, A, A, A, and Left.

Team Big Players: Press Z, B, B, B, B, A, and Right.

No Punting: Press Z, B, B, B, B, B, A, and Up.

Big Head: Press Z, Z, and Right.

Team Big Head: Press Z, Z, A, A, A, and Right.

No First Downs: Press Z, Z, B, and Up.

Allow Stepping Out of Bounds: Press Z, Z, B, A, and Left.

Power-up Teammates: Press Z, Z, B, B, B, A, A, A, and Up.

Fast Passing: Press Z, Z, B, B, B, B, B, and Left.

Team Tiny Players: Press Z, Z, Z, B, and Right.

Power-up Blockers: Press Z, Z, Z, B, A, A, and Left.

Power-up Offense: Press Z, Z, Z, B, A, A, and Up.

Smart CPU Opponent: Press Z, Z, Z, B, A, A, A, A, and Down. Great for one-player game only.

No Interceptions: Press Z, Z, Z, B, B, B, B, A, A, A, A, and Up.

Power-up Speed: Press Z, Z, Z, Z, A, A, A, A, and Left. In a two-player game, both players must enter the code.

Power-up Defense: Press Z, Z, Z, Z, A, A, B, and Up.

No Random Fumbles: Press Z, Z, Z, Z, A, A, B, B, B, and Down.

Turn Off Stadium: Press Z, Z, Z, Z, Z, and Left.

Infinite Turbo: Press Z, Z, Z, Z, Z, B, A, A, A, A, and Up.

Rain: Press Z, Z, Z, Z, Z, B, B, B, B, B, A, A, A, A, A, and Right.

EXAMPLE B

At the Match-Up or Versus screen, press Turbo (for the first number), Jump (for the second number), and Pass (for the third number) as shown to activate the codes. The numbers in the following cheat codes list indicate the number of times each button should be pressed. Then press the directional pad in the direction indicated to complete the code.

Code	Action
<u>Code</u>	<u>Action</u>
010 Up	Late hits
040 Up	Huge head
045 Up	Super blitzing
151 Up	No punting
210 Up	No first downs
233 Up	Power-up teammates
312 Up	Power-up offense
344 Up	No interceptions
421 Up	Power-up defense
433 Up	Invisible
514 Up	Infinite turbo
555 Up	Hyper blitz (two-player agreement needed)
021 Right	Show more field (two-player agreement needed)
050 Right	Big football
102 Right	Hide receiver name
123 Right	Headless team
141 Right	Team big players
200 Right	Big head
203 Right	Team big heads

Code	Action
222 Right	Night game
310 Right	Team tiny players
555 Right	Weather: rain
001 Down	Show field goal %
012 Down	No CPU assistance (two-player agreement needed)
030 Down	Fog on
041 Down	Thick fog on
111 Down	Tournament mode (only in two-player game)
232 Down	Ground fog on
314 Down	Smart CPU opponent (only for single-player game)
423 Down	No random fumbles
525 Down	Weather: snow
032 Left	Fast turbo running
115 Left	No play selection (two-player agreement needed)
123 Left	Super field goals
211 Left	Allow stepping out of bounds
250 Left	Fast passes

Code	Action
212 Left	Weather: clear
312 Left	Power-up blockers
321 Left	No head
333 Left	Invisible receiver highlight
342 Left	Super quarterbacks
404 Left	Power-up speed (two-player agreement needed)
500 Left	Turn off stadium

THE BEST OF THE REST: FOOTBALL

GAME NAME: MADDEN 64

ESRB RATING: E for Everyone. Content suitable for those 6 years or older.

THEME: Professional football

PLAYERS: 1 to 4

DEVELOPED BY: Electronic Arts

COMMENTS: A realistic football game with a ton of secret codes, which makes it great. The codes aren't just goofy, either. You can unlock some of the classic teams that go all the way back to the 1960s.

Secret Stats Team: To access this team of Stat Leaders, go to the season mode and select Front

Office. Then go to Create Player and enter "STATS MEN" as the player name. Save the name as you would a normal player and exit. Note: Works only in exhibition mode.

Electronic Arts Team: To access this team of Stat Leaders, go to the season mode and select Front Office. Then go to Create Player and enter "ELEC ARTS" as the player name. Save the name as you would a normal player and exit. Note: Works only in exhibition mode. Another note: The EA team is huge and members have amazing skill levels.

Electronic Arts Stadium: To access this stadium, go to the season mode and select Front Office. Then go to Create Player and enter "SAN MATEO" as the player name. Save the name as you would a normal player and exit. Note: Works only in exhibition mode.

Tiburon Stadium: To access this stadium, go to the season mode and select Front Office. Then go to Create Player and enter "MAITLAND" as the player name. Save the name as you would a normal player and exit. Note: Works only in exhibition mode.

Classic Codes:

The 60s Conference B Team: Enter season mode and head to Front Office. Now choose Create Player and enter "SIXTIES" in the space for player names. Save the team/player you created. Press B, B to return to the Menu screen. The team will be available for exhibition mode.

The All 70s Team Conference B Team: Enter season mode and head to Front Office. Now choose Create Player and enter ''SEVENTIES'' in the space for player names. Save the team/player you created. Press B, B to return to the Menu screen. The team will be available for exhibition mode.

All 80s Team: Enter season mode and head to Front Office. Now choose Create Player and enter ''EIGHTIES'' in the space for player names. Save the team/player you created. Press B, B to return to the Menu screen. The team will be available for exhibition mode.

More Recent Team Codes:

97 NFC Pro Bowl Team: Enter season mode and head to Front Office. Now choose Create Player and enter ''LEI'' in the space for player names. Save the team/player you created. Press B, B to return to the Menu screen. The team will be available for exhibition mode.

97 AFC Pro Bowl Team: Enter season mode and head to Front Office. Now choose Create Player and enter ''HOWLIE'' in the space for player names. Save the team/player you created. Press B, B to return to the Menu screen. The team will be available for exhibition mode.

Madden All Time Team: Enter season mode and head to Front Office. Now choose Create Player and enter ''ATMADDEN'' in the space for player names. Save the team/player you created. Press B, B to return to the Menu screen. The team will be available for exhibition mode.

Showing Off: When you have a player completely clear and coming into the end zone, press Down and hold C-Left. He'll high-step into a touchdown.

GAME NAME: **NFL QUARTERBACK CLUB 99**

ESRB RATING: **E for Everyone. Content suitable for those 6 years or older.**

THEME: **Professional football**

PLAYERS: **1 to 4**

DEVELOPED BY: **Iguana**

PUBLISHED BY: **Acclaim**

COMMENTS: There are unbelievable graphics in this realistic football game. This game is a must for any serious football fan. Also, check out the codes the designers gave the different features, some of which are really funny: like ''BTTRFNGRS'' for butterfingers to access frequent fumbling and ''HSPTL'' for Hospital for the frequent injury code. Also *X-Files* fans should appreciate "SCLLYMLDR" (Scully and Mulder) for the Alien Stadium. Hey, who says that programmers don't have a sense of humor?

Codes:

The following codes should be entered from the game's easily accessible Cheat menu.

Action	Code
Alien Stadium	SCLLYMLDR
Always Fumble	BTTRFNGRS
Big Coin at the Toss	BGMNY
Big Football	BCHBLL
Cheat/Hidden Teams	XTRTMS
Double Downs	DBLDWNS
Electric Football	XTRVLTG
Fat Players	MRSHMLLW
Fire Ball	HSNFR
Flubber Ball	FLBBR
Huge Pylons	PWRPYLNS
Injury-prone Players	HSPTL
Land Mines on the Field	PPCRNRTRNS

Action	Code
No Fumbles	STCKYBLL
Pinball Players That Bounce Around	PNBLL
Raquetball Mode	RCQTBLL
Rugby Mode	RGBY
Skinny Players	TTHPCK
Slippery Mode	SLPNSLD
Slow-motion Play	FRRSTGMP
Super Kickers	PWRKCKR
Unlimited	TRBMN

SOCCER

GAME NAME: FIFA 99

ESRB RATING: E for Everyone. Content suitable for those 6 years or older.

THEME: Soccer

PLAYERS: 1 to 2

DEVELOPED BY: Electronic Arts Sports

COMMENTS: Every European country worth thinking about is here in FIFA 99 (even France). So, you're not only playing for glory, but all those cool international trophies as well.

Features include multidirectional chest control and semiautomatic goalies. (Users can choose when the goalie should charge an attacker.)

Players have choices of modes: a standard season of league games: The Champions' League; the Winners' Cup; and the EA-created European Super League with 20 different teams. Use the professional difficulty level and win the Champions' Cup as Brazil.

A real cool feature is that players are of different sizes so it takes a while to get used to them. Also, play is more realistic than previous soccer games. For instance, a player can now change direction in midturn. This may seem like a small thing, but the video wizard who masters it first has a real advantage. In other games, players had to complete a turn before changing directions, so if you're still playing that way reflexively or don't know about this new feature, then you're at a real disadvantage—at least for a few goals until you learn what's going on. Another thing to learn is that players can stop and start more quickly than in previous soccer games, so plan your strategy accordingly.

So you've mastered the game and you want to beat up on a new player. Here's a good strategy to show your opponent. The goalie is controllable. You can bring him out of the net. The person who learns this first is going to abuse it and let the opponent score while scrambling to get back to the goal. So, get the controllable goalie out of your system while playing against the computer, then show a newcomer the feature and he'll leave the net open for you.

THE BEST OF THE REST: SOCCER

GAME NAME: **FIFA SOCCER 64**

ESRB RATING: **E for Everyone. Content suitable for those 6 years or older.**

THEME: **Soccer**

PLAYERS: **1 to 4**

DEVELOPED BY: **Electronic Arts Sports**

COMMENTS: **Authentic 3D soccer action. Great for serious soccer fans.**

NOISE CODES: These noises are available only after a goal is scored, but you can use them as often as you like until the kickoff.

Exhibit Bad Sportsmanship: Press the control pad in any direction during game play and the crowd will boo. Only available once per quarter . . . Boooo!

Sound Effects Following Goal: Air horn: C-Up to play an air horn.

Another Air Horn: C-Right.

Play Drum: C-Down

Play a Different Drum: C-Left

GAME NAME: **FIFA: ROAD TO THE WORLD CUP 98**

ESRB RATING: **E for Everyone. Content suitable for those 6 years or older.**

THEME: **Soccer**

PLAYERS: **1 to 2**

DEVELOPED BY: **Electronic Arts Sports**

COMMENTS: Another soccer game with great 3-D action for serious fans.

Codes:

Upside-Down Mode (sometimes called the Down Under Australian Mode): Go to the Player Edit screen and select the Australian team from Zone 2-OFC Conference. Then enter ''NWO-DEDISPU'' to rename the first player. The screen will now be upside down.

Transparent Players: Select Slovakia (Zone 4-UEFA Conference) and enter ''LASKO'' as the first player name. If entered correctly, the player on the screen will jump and others will be invisible.

Hot Potato Mode: Select Rep. Ireland (Zone 4-UEFA Conference) and enter ''SPUD'' as the first player name. Nothing much will happen at first, but at random times during the game players will kick the ball and the team will fall down.

No Out of Bounds: Choose the Wales team (Zone 4-UEFA Conference) and enter "WARREN" as the first player name. This will surround the field with invisible walls and the ball will not be able to go out of bounds. Great for practice or really young players.

Player Points (Unlimited Skill Points): While on the Player Edit screen enter "DAVE" as the name of the first player in the Vancouver team (USA Conference).

Round Select: Change the name of the first player to "YUJI" on Japan's team (Zone 3-AFC Conference). This will enable you to bypass any round on your way to the World Cup.

Victory Scenes: Name the first player from Japan (Zone 3-AFC Conference) "NORIE" and go into the World Cup mode. When you get to the Round Select screen, press Z and then C-Left and C-Up all at once. You'll see a cool animated celebration.

Invisible Players: Go to Player Edit and select ScheffieldW. Then enter "WAYNE" as a player name.

Pencil and Paper Mode: Go to Player Edit and select Canada. Then enter "MARC" as a player name.

Delete Stadium: Go to Player Edit and select any team. Then enter "CATCH22" as a player name.

Small Players: Go to Player Edit and select Vancouver. Then enter "KERRY" as a player name.

GAME NAME: **INTERNATIONAL SUPERSTAR SOCCER 64**

ESRB RATING: **E for Everyone. Content suitable for those 6 years or older.**

THEME: **Soccer**

PLAYERS: **1 to 4**

DEVELOPED BY: **Konami**

COMMENTS: A lot of realistic action and great player choices. Truthfully, I don't like soccer games that much, but this one is pretty good.

Secret All Star Teams: When Press Start comes up on the screen, use the control pad to press Up L, Up L, Down L, Down L, Left R, Right R, Left R, Right R, B, and A. Then hold down the Z button. (Got that? It takes a little practice.) Then press Start. The announcer will say "What an incredible comeback!" Now, go to open game and penalty kick modes and you'll see a new group of teams. These are the All Stars, which include Euro Stars A, Euro Stars B, Asian Stars, African Stars, All American Stars, and World Stars.

Big Heads: When Press Start comes up on the screen, press C-Up, C-Up, C-Down, C-Down, C-Left, C-Right, C-Left, C-Right, B, and A. Then hold down Z and press Start. The big heads will appear when you start a match.

HOCKEY

GAME NAME: NHL 99

ESRB RATING: E for Everyone. Content suitable for those 6 years or older.

THEME: Professional hockey

PLAYERS: 1 to 4

DEVELOPED BY: Electronic Arts/EA Sports

COMMENTS: Here's hockey action so real you can almost feel your teeth getting smashed out as you play. NHL 99 features six modes of play, from beginner, which features a more relaxed game without coaching strategies, line changes, and penalties, to a full season, which ends in the Stanley Cup. Naturally, all 27 NHL teams are supplied along with enough options to create dream teams and weird teams. As for the arenas themselves, they are as detailed as anything you'll find. Take a moment out from the action to check out the center ice logos, championship banners, and luxury boxes. There's also the option of either a 26- or 82-game season that goes into the playoffs, though those less patient can hit the playoffs right away for a series that can last from one to seven games. There is even a quick start mode, which features a video rematch of the Detroit Red Wings and Washington Capitals from the '98 Stanley Cup.

Other modes of play include an Olympic mode where you play for bronze, silver, and gold honors and a shoot-out mode where you can go one-on-one as either goalie or shooter. And yes, you can check, fight, and skate backward.

Now, here's the thing: Former Colorado Avalanche coach Marc Crawford (Remember him? Stanley Cup winner in '96 ring any bells?) designed the strategies for the game, and they are good. You get to them from the Strategy menu in the Start menu. However, you are not locked into the strategies he provides. The Strategy menu contains controls for offensive and defensive pressure. If you naturally play offensively, then you can turn the offensive pressure down a bit and the defensive pressure up. Get it? You're going to have to practice to find your best levels, but the extra effort is worth it.

The other option you have is to switch your goalie from CPU/computer-controlled to manual controls. There's no real advantage to this in actual play. In fact, the CPU-controlled goalie is very, very good. However, if you enjoy the goalie spot, then this is the kind of thing you'll want to do. The way to get control of the goalie is to go to the Set-Up screen and press Left/Right on the control stick to get the icon into the field of the team you wish to play. Now press C-Up to toggle the goalie to manual control.

Okay, not that you'd ever want to start a fight on purpose—not while playing hockey! But hey, fights happen, right? So, in the spirit of *avoiding* fights during your play of NHL 99, I'll tell you how a fight *might* break out. Suppose a player from your team who rates high in aggressiveness as an attribute repeatedly bodychecks a player from the opposing team who also rates high in aggressiveness. Then you might have a fight on your hands. So, now you know how to avoid fights, right? Never ever have one of your highly aggressive players bodycheck a highly aggressive opponent.

However, if by some quirk of fate, luck, or accident your player does repeatedly check that other player and a fight does break out, then never ever hit the A button, because that would cause your man to throw a hook-type punch. Also, be sure not to hit the B button, because that would send a jab to the opponent's jaw. And whatever you do, don't push C, because that would cause your player to grab the other player's jersey. Got it? Now, repeat after me, "I will never have my player check an opponent again and again to start a fight. Though if by chance a rare fight does occur on the ice, then I will never ever use the A, B, B, B, B, A, B, B, B, A, C combination.''

The other thing you never want to do is take unfair advantage of someone who knows nothing about hockey, right? I mean, suppose some teams were just better than other teams in the league. That would mean you could pick the best team and have your opponent pick the worst team. You'd have an unfair advantage, right? Well, for the benefit of those who are simply curious, the programmers made the Detroit Red Wings the best team in the NHL while the U.S. and Canadian teams are the best in the national competitions. Teams that you might want to give to an opponent are: New York Islanders, Boston Bruins, Ottawa Senators, Tampa Bay Lightning, Nashville Predators, and Los Angeles Kings.

Now, the last bit of advice on hockey's good sportsmanship tradition. After making a goal, it's always good to act dignified, quiet, and never ever make your opponent feel bad that he didn't score a goal. After all, it doesn't matter who scored a goal as long as somebody on some team did. Dignity, sophistication, and good sportsmanship are long traditions in the game of hockey.

With that said, you should be very careful after scoring a goal. Put your controller down and quietly watch the replay while congratulating your opponent on a good effort. Whatever you do, avoid hitting the Z button on the controller when the auto-replay is running after a goal. If you hit the Z button after a goal, noises will come up. And if you pick one of the noises and hold the Z button, then your opponent's rumble pak will activate. And this could make him feel bad about the goal you scored.

One other strategy tip is that regardless of how good you are on other hockey games, be warned that the creases are smaller on this unit. No, there isn't a crease shortage, but rather a change in NHL rules that make the real creases smaller, too.

The game includes a whole bunch of different strategies, but I'm not going into each and every one of them. However, the best choice for the beginner is the Combination. Using the Combination strategy, the CPU will select the best offense based on moment-to-moment play and your opponent's choice of strategy. When playing offense, the Combination strategy program sets up your men in the best set-up possible to counter your opponent's defense. When playing in the defensive position, it sets up a basic Zone Defense, leaving your man to take on the puck-handler.

Codes:

There are plenty of codes in NHL, all of them pretty good. To enter a code go to the Option screen and highlight the word Password. Then enter:

Code	Action
BIGBIG	Makes your players big.
BRAINY	Makes your players' heads big.
FAST	Gives you faster game play.
FASTER	Gives you, what else, even faster game play.
PULLED	Takes goalies out of the game. It's an easier game, but it also takes your goalie. So, use cautiously.
FLASH	Adds camera flashes to the crowd.
VICTORY	Gives you a view of the ending sequence.
3RD	Gives selected teams a third set of jerseys, if you're into making a fashion statement while playing hockey.

THE BEST OF THE REST: HOCKEY

GAME NAME: WAYNE GRETZKY'S 3D HOCKEY '98
ESRB RATING: E for Everyone. Content suitable for those 6 years or older.
THEME: Realistic hockey
PLAYERS: 1 to 4
DEVELOPED BY: Midway
COMMENTS: There are some great secret codes in this game. There are codes that relate to actual

hockey for the fans and some really weird ones for those who just like to mess with the video characters.

Fighting: At the Options screen, hold the L shift button and press the following buttons: C-Up, C-Up, C-Down, C-Left, C-Right, C-Right, C-Left, C-Right, C-Left. The game will begin as usual, but the players will be extra sensitive and start fights at the drop of a hat-trick.

Secret Teams: This code activates four Super Teams: Canada, USA, 99ers, and Williams. On the Option screen, before you've picked your team, hold the L button and enter the following sequence on your C buttons: C-Right, C-Left, C-Left, C-Right, C-Left, C-Left, C-Right, C-Left, and C-Left. Then go to the Team Select screen and look for an additional conference that includes the four new teams.

Fun with Codes: Go to the Options menu and press C-Up, C-Left (or C-Down) and then press R shift. You'll see a collection of numbers that are called Specials. The first six digits of these numbers determine what a player will look like in a game. Play around with them to get different looks.

Player and Rink Size: Suppose you're not happy with the player or rink size. Okay, suppose you're just bored with playing the same old game. Or suppose you really want to have a good laugh. Here's the code: Go to the Option screen. Hold the C-Down and press the R button. This will bring up a line of zeros at the bottom of the screen with ''Specials'' written next to them. C-Down and Shift-R changes the first two digits. C-Left and Shift-R changes the third and fourth digits. C-Up and Shift-R changes the fifth and sixth digits.

Big Head Size: Press C-Down and hold Shift-R until the first two digits are 10.

Even Bigger Head Size: Press C-Down and hold Shift-R until the first two digits are 01.

Small Head Size: Press C-Down and hold Shift-R until the first two digits are 11.

Tiny Players: Hold down C-Left and Shift-R until the third digit is 1.

Big Huge Players: Hold down C-Left and Shift-R until the fourth digit is 1.

Short Fat Players: Hold down C-Up and Shift-R until the fifth digit is 1.

Tall Skinny Players: Hold down C-Up and Shift-R until the sixth digit is 1.

Be Creative: Also, you should play around with the numbers and mix and match different codes.

You can get some really weird-looking players—for instance, Tall Skinny Players with humongous heads.

Fun with Advertising: Go to the Options menu and press Z to look at an ad. Whenever you press Z, another ad appears. Okay, so it's not a lot of fun, but you can teach it to a four-year-old and he'll think you're really cool.

GAME NAME: NAGANO OLYMPIC HOCKEY '98

ESRB RATING: E for Everyone. Content suitable for those 6 years or older.

THEME: Olympic hockey

PLAYERS: 1 to 4

PUBLISHED BY: Midway

COMMENTS: The Nagano Winter Olympics of 1998 are now just a memory, or would be a memory if I had actually watched them. But that doesn't matter because one good thing that came out of the Olympics was a solid sports game: Nagano Olympic Hockey '98.

Because it's based on the same software engine used in the two Gretzky games, Nagano Olympic hockey plays much like those two. In fact, it also has a lot of the same codes as the Gretzky games. So, if you're at the local video store and want to rent Gretzky but it's out, then check this baby out. It plays almost exactly the same. However, the familiar NHL franchises have been replaced by nations, so you have 14 different countries competing for the gold. These teams are the United States, Austria, Canada, Finland, France, Germany, Italy, Japan, Russia, Sweden, Belarus, Czech Republic, Kazakhstan, and Slovakia. Yeah, be the first one to play as Slovakia.

There's two play modes: single game and Olympic mode, which means you play a trio of qualifying matches to compete in the eight team finals. However, you can also skip the prelims and go to the finals, too.

There's also trading, but the game calls them *defections*. However, you can only replace goalies with other goalies. All the other positions are up for grabs by anyone. Centers, wings, and defensive men are all interchangeable.

One of the coolest features is that you can change 14 different things about the skaters, including face, weight, number, speed, et cetera. This is a very, very interesting game feature if you want to have, say, a team of 300-pound French guys playing 98-pound Slovakians. This feature doesn't, however, last into the actual game play. But it is great for a laugh.

Codes:

Following are some of the easier codes.

Announcer's Voice: To give the announcer a deeper voice, hold C-Up and press R. Repeat to give him a high voice.

Body and Head Sizes: Go to the Options screen and hold C-Down and press R. A message will appear at the screen's bottom. Now you can do a head-size change by holding C-Down and selecting the size. To change body type, hold C-Left and press R. The same code works for players' height.

Fight Time: To raise the fight-ability of your players, go to the Options screen and hold down the L button.

Goalie Hit: To smash the goalie come in on the net at full speed in a straight line. Then press Shoot, Pass, and Turbo buttons at the same time. The goalie will fly back into the net.

More Codes:

In order to work the best codes, you have to go into the debug mode. To get there: Go to the Options screen and press C-Down and R-Shift, then C-Left and R-Shift. (It may also work with C-Up and R-Shift.) Now you should see the 16-digit codes. They are called "Specials." Please note, you can change only the first six digits.

Code	Player Change
100000	Fat Players
010000	Fat Players with Big Giant Heads

Code	Player Change
110000	Fat Players with Teeny-Tiny Heads
001000	Teeny-Tiny Players and Itsy-Bitsy Announcer
000100	Huge Giant Players and Huge Giant Announcer
000010	Scrunched and Crunched Players and Teeny-Tiny Announcer
010101	Big Giant Players with Huge Heads and Big Giant Announcer
000001	Tall Stringbean Players and Big Giant Announcer
110110	Big Giant Players with Itsy-Bitsy Heads and Giant Announcer
010010	Scrunched and Crunched Players with Big Giant Heads, Teeny-Tiny Announcer

NOTE: The words Teeny Tiny, Itsy Bitsy, Big Giant, and Stringbean appear nowhere in the game. They are highly technical terms. And if you don't believe me, then you're a Doody Head.

NOTE: The word Doody Head is another technical term used frequently by video game programmers to show their displeasure.

BASEBALL

GAME NAME: ALL STAR BASEBALL '99

ESRB RATING: E for Everyone. Content suitable for those 6 years or older.

THEME: Take a guess

PLAYERS: 1 to 4

DEVELOPED BY: Acclaim/Iguana

COMMENTS: This is a game that'll take you out to the ballgame. Even if you can't stand baseball because it's long, boring, and filled with about as much action as watching paint dry, this game is very entertaining. Suppose you love baseball in a big way? Then you're in luck, because there is enough realism here to keep even the most die-hard, stat-obsessed fan going. Plus, there are also digitized photos of most of the players. And Yankees' radio announcers Michael Kay and John Sterling provide play-by-play and commentary. There's also color commentary.

First off, you can play as long as you want.

That means you can choose to play everything from a single exhibition game (terrific way to practice) or a full 162-game season. Or you can just skip the whole thing and head right to the playoffs or World Series. Oh, if only we could program the real teams like that! And for those players with really short attention spans (you know who you are), there is a Home Run Derby feature that puts four American League batters against four National League sluggers.

A load of realism is packed into this game. For instance, night games, twilight games, and day games. The effects are so real you can even see the players' shadows on the field. There are also choices for different weather conditions. But just how real are the stadiums? Glad you asked. The game includes all 30 big-league ballparks, and the stadiums are so real that those that really have Jumbotrons to display an image of the action on the field have them in the game. Now, that's real.

What if you hate baseball and baseball video games? All I can say is, if you hate baseball and baseball videos that much, then you probably have something against apple pie, too! Okay, maybe you're not dangerous, just different. Maybe you like to mix up your baseball video games with a little goofiness? Then this is the baseball game for you. All-Star Baseball '99 features a bunch—a big, huge bunch—of codes you can punch in to play against aliens (the team is called the Abductors) or change the appearance of your team. This comes in real handy if you're playing someone who isn't into the whole stat, team-building, manager thing. You also can choose between Simulation and a fast-paced Arcade mode. Plus, while playing against the CPU, you can choose a difficulty level of Rookie, Veteran, or All-Star. This choice is key for developing strategy. Every player should spend at least some time at the Rookie level getting buttoning moves and strategy down.

Now, for you baseball fanatics. Yeah, you guys who want to play the full 162-game season mode. There's a team manager option that can't be beat. You can call up players from the Triple A team, trade players, and even draft free agents. There is also an option that allows you to create your own custom players. However, be warned: you can't put together another Babe Ruth. The game automatically puts a limit on how much baseball skill you can give to a custom player.

Tips:

When going up against a strong opponent, turn off the pitching cursor. The rumble pak will warn you when your aim is out of the strike zone.

Whenever you create a player, choose a slugger with a crouched batting stance to give him a smaller strike zone. Don't worry, this will not hurt his hitting abilities.

When bunting, be sure to bunt down the third base line. Fielders for the CPU have trouble getting the runner out at first.

When you're pitching, the CPU has a runner on base, and you need another out, delay pitching the ball for a while. The runner will come off the base in a long, long lead. When the lead gets as long as it can, then throw to the base. Most of the time he will be called out. This takes a little practice, but it's a good easy out. I've found it works best when the runner is on first. When the CPU has a runner on second, wait for him to go past the ump before trying to throw him out. It also works best when there is only a single runner on base. I've found that the best way to do this is to press A to pitch and then, before the pitcher releases, press C.

You can get more power behind a hit by holding the joystick down when swinging.

When first starting out, use the ball marker from the Game Options. Yeah, yeah, yeah, I know you can hit a mile, but hitting can be particularly tricky in this game, so you should get it down cold with the marker before going it alone. Believe me, it will help on control and distance. Lock the doors, turn down the sound, and play the game under a blanket if you're embarrassed about using the marker, but use it. You'll be thankful you did in the long run.

Codes:

At the Cheat screen, enter ''ATEMYBUIK'' to play the alien abduction mode. After entering the code, start an Exhibition or Quick Play, select a stadium, and scroll to the bottom to Alienapolis Park. The home team will have the same stats as the team that was picked during set-up but the players will now look like aliens. ''GOTHELIUM'' will produce the big head, hands, feet, and bat feature. ''PRPPAPLYR'' makes the player extremely thin, like paper. ''GRTBLSFDST'' makes the ball trail smoke along its path.

When playing in the Kansas City Royals' Kauffman Stadium, hit one of the two signs that read ''WIN A LIZARD'' and your team is turned into ball-playing lizards.

Any of the following codes can be entered during the game. Press the following key commands in the game.

Code	Result
URARADDUUD	Paper-thin players
LARDBALL	Big extremities—head, hands, feet, even bats
URALLBULL	Big baseball

Code   Result

ALLRUBR   Fat and skinny players

THE BEST OF THE REST: BASEBALL

GAME NAME: MAJOR LEAGUE BASEBALL FEATURING KEN GRIFFEY, JR.

ESRB RATING: E for Everyone. Content suitable for those 6 years or older.

THEME: Again, I bet you can guess this

PLAYERS: 1 or 2

DEVELOPED BY: Angel Studios

PUBLISHED BY: Nintendo

COMMENTS: So, maybe it's winter outside and there's snow on the ground. Baseball season is months away. What to do? What to do? Well, you can either hit pop-ups in the living room or pop this baby into your system: a one- or two-player game with great pitching and hitting control. Also, there are a bunch of serious and silly codes.

Codes:

Call a Homer: When Griffey comes up to the plate, press Left, Left, Right, Right, Right, Left, Left. Griffey will point his bat. If you hit the very next pitch, it will be a home run.

Dancing Batter and Pitcher: No, they do not dance together! Dancing Batter and Pitcher works for either batter or pitcher. Press Up, Up, Down, Left, Left, Right, Right, Left, Left, Down, Up, Up before a pitch is thrown.

Fireworks: At the Stadium Select screen, press Z to check out the stadium, then Z-Right to shoot fireworks.

Secret Teams: Select an exhibition game and hold all four C buttons down. You should hear a confirmation tone. Then go to the All-Star Teams screen. The secret teams should be listed there.

Spin the Ball: While on the title screen, hold down the Z button. The baseball will stop rotating. Then use the pad to move the ball around.

Win the World Series: Go to the exhibition game, pick your teams, and then go to the Stadium Select screen. Press all four C buttons and Z. Fireworks and game credits will roll.

GAME NAME: **MIKE PIAZZA'S STRIKE ZONE**
ESRB RATING: **E for Everyone. Content suitable for those 6 years or older.**
THEME: **Professional baseball, again**
PLAYERS: **1 or 2**

DEVELOPED BY: **Devil's Thumb Entertainment**

COMMENTS: All 30 big-league teams and stadiums and some really wild codes.

Codes:

Sky Color: Go to the Today's Game screen and enter C, A, Z, C-Up, L, R, Z.

Hidden Stadium: On the Today's Game screen, press L, R, L, and R to make the cursor disappear. Press Right, A, C-Up, L, and A. Press Start. Then start the game. When the field powers up, you'll be in the Devil's Thumb Stadium.

Crazy Pitching: On the Today's Game screen, press L, R, L, and R to make the cursor disappear. Press C-Right, A, Z, C-Up, R, B. Press Start to make the cursor reappear. Every ball will come at the plate in a weird pattern.

Crazy Hitting: On the Today's Game screen, press L, R, L, and R to make the cursor disappear. Press C-Right, A, Z, B, A, L, L. Press Start to make the cursor reappear. When the ball is hit, it'll bounce around like a Ping-Pong ball.

Aluminum Bats: When the game is in play, press Start to pause the game. Then enter R, L, R, B, L, B, and A on the Today's Game screen.

Red Bats: When the game is in play, press Start to pause the game. Then enter L, R, L, R, R, Down, B, and A on the Today's Game screen.

Multicolored Bats: When the game is in play, press Start to pause the game. Then enter L, R, L, R, B, L, B, and A on the Today's Game screen.

All Pitch Options and Modes: When the game is in play, press Start to pause the game. Then enter L, R, L, R, C-Right, A, Z, C-Up, R, and L on the Today's Game screen.

Announcer Weirdness: Just as the MLB insignia comes up on the screen, press C-Up, R, B, B. (Note: At your own risk.)

Easy Homers: On the Today's Game screen, press L, R, L, and R. Then press L, A, Down on the joypad, C-Up, and R.

Easy Steals: On the Today's Game screen, press L, R, L, R. Then press C-Left, A, down on the joypad, C-Up, Z.

SNOWBOARDING

GAME NAME: 1080°

ESRB RATING: E for Everyone. Content suitable for those 6 years or older.

THEME: Extreme snowboarding

PLAYERS: 1 or 2

DEVELOPED BY: Nintendo

COMMENTS AND CODES: Here it is, the chance to snowboard without getting cold, wet, or stupid. Not to say that all extreme sports types are dumb, it's just that some of them make hockey players look like Harvard graduates. And that's not to say that hockey players are stupid; some of them make football players look like honor roll students. I could go on like this, but why bother? You get the idea.

In case you didn't know, 1080° (ten-eighty) refers to the snowboarding move of three 360° turns in midair. Okay, so maybe I was wrong, snowboarders can do some math.

At first glance you may think going down a

hill on a piece of wood is not a real great time. Maybe it's fun in real life, but how much action could there be in a video game, right? Wrong. 1080° is a whole bunch of fun, thanks to the folks at Nintendo.

1080° has six different courses/modes. Crystal Lake, Crystal Peak, Golden Forest and Mountain Village are the regular play modes. Then there are two bonus tracks. Dragon Cave opens only after you beat all *five* courses on Hard setting. To run the second secret course you have to beat the six courses on Expert setting.

What makes the game a long-term pleaser is that there are a blizzard of options and modes to play. The play options are broken down three ways: Compete against the computer, compete for time, and compete for points earned for board tricks. (Tip: The absolute best way to rack up points on tricks is to learn the combos. Combos are the ability to do more than one trick at a time.)

What you want to do is go to the Training course first. That's where you'll learn the major boarding tricks and buttoning sequences. This is really important. There are something like 25 tricks to learn, and you have to get good at all of them to be halfway decent at the game. You also can earn some of the secret modes there, but more on that later. You have a choice between two courses here, a long relatively flat run and a hazardous, really steep run with a bunch of jumps. In order to compete against the machine and friends, spend time on each of these courses. You'll be glad you did.

Then there's the match race mode, where you take on the CPU-controlled opponent over a variety of courses, lighting effects, and weather conditions.

In time attack, you try to beat the clock. Actually, time attack is a great practice mode for mastering the courses before playing against an actual live person.

Trick attack is also a great way to practice, particularly those less than easy board tricks. You're playing for points earned for performing tricks, so there's reason to try very risky stunts. This is a great place to master your combo moves.

Contest mode is a variation of both trick attack and time attack. The object is to perform as many tricks as possible against the clock. Another good practice mode before taking on your friends.

And, finally, of course, the versus mode. This two-player mode puts you head-to-head with your buddies. This is where 1080° is at it's best.

There are five boarders to choose from at the opening of the game. Each has his own attributes and specialties.

Kensuke Kimachi: Designated by Nintendo as the best all-around boarder, he's a good choice for beginners.

Ricky Winterborn: Excellent at jumping

tricks but not very fast. He's a natural for the trick attack mode. Winterborn's main talent is going for air, not speed. His primary characteristic is that he is matchless at technical and jumping skills. This makes him an excellent choice for freestyle events.

Rob Haywood: What Winterborn lacks in speed, Haywood more than makes up for. So, he's your time attack guy. However, Haywood isn't a great trickster, and his jumping skills are definitely not up to Winterborn's.

Akari Hayami: The only girl on the team, she can go either way. She is not the fastest or the most agile boarder, though she is pretty good on the jumps.

Dion Blaster: The fastest boarder of the crew and a great candidate for time attack, but watch out if you get him on a jump. He is definitely below the others in terms of tricks.

There are also four hidden boarders, Panda, Ice Man, Crystal Boarder, and Gold Ice Man. To play as Panda, you have to beat the preset scores for time attack and trick attack modes. Then go to the Rider Selection screen and choose Haywood. Press C-Right and A. The Panda will come up in Haywood's place. Then go to training mode to learn his special tricks. To play as Ice Man, you have to win the Match Race on the Expert level and beat all the preset scores in trick attack and time attack modes. No easy stunt, but it's worth it. Really. Go to any mode from the Options menu and then go to the screen with Akari's stats. While checking out her stats, hold C-Left and then A. To get Crystal Boarder, win at the expert level in Match Race, then go back to Player Selection, highlight Hayami, and press C-Left and A. To get the Gold Ice Man, you have to beat Match Race on the Expert level. After doing this—no sweat, right?—go to Kensuke's stats and press C-Up, A, then let go of C-Up. This is a tough one but definitely worth it. The Gold Ice Man is the best and the baddest, the all-around kick-butt boarder in the game.

Now, there are a whole wall of boards to choose from in 1080°. In fact, there are eight. All of them have different attributes and rider compatibility. Do yourself a favor, *always pick the Tahoe 151*. It is without a doubt the best all-around board for tricks, speed, and jumps.

There's one other trick you should know about: the penguin board. Much different from a bored penguin, the penguin board is available only after you've completed all the tricks in the training mode. After you've done all the tricks, go back to the game and take a look at the wall with the snowboards and choose the Tahoe 151 and press C-Down. Not much will happen; in fact, nothing will change. However, when you go to the course, you'll be riding a penguin.

Tips:

Suppose you want to complete all 24 tricks in the training mode but stink at them. Okay, maybe you don't stink at all of them, just a few. Hey, these aren't easy tricks, so we'll give you a break. Here's how you can get around mastering the hardest tricks. As you perform an easy trick in training, quickly press C-Right to get back to the Trick menu. Then change your selection to whatever trick you can't perform. The CPU will credit you with the tougher trick.

Suppose you want to choose whom you race against when competing against the CPU. Easy to do. Choose the mode, then when the race begins, press Start, then Restart. You can do this until the exact opponent you want comes up.

So maybe you love that flying stuff, but every time you come down you land on your butt. Hey, that's no fun, right? When coming in for a landing, make sure your board is lined up with the ground, then ease back a little and just before you land go into a crouch by pressing Z. This will also keep you from skidding out of control. This trick can be a major help when landing after completing a high-flying spin. If you're landing on an uneven surface, then tilt the board to match the surface.

You can get a quick start from the starting line by pressing Up twice on the joystick just as the announcer shouts "Go!" This trick also works when going through deep snow.

THE BEST OF THE REST: SNOWBOARDING

GAME NAME: **SNOWBOARD KIDS**

ESRB RATING: **E for Everyone. Content suitable for those 6 years or older.**

THEME: **Snowboarding**

PLAYERS: **1 to 4**

DEVELOPED BY: **Racdym**

PUBLISHED BY: **Altus Software**

COMMENTS: A lot of snow and a lot of boards. Okay, seriously, the controls are easier to manage and there's more to do than in other snowboard racing games like collect gold coins and stuff. There's also a cool battle mode where you can shoot at your friends as well as a time attack mode. So, if you find some of the other snowboard games kind of boring, then you might want to give this one a try.

Tip:

Turbo Boost: Start tapping on the A button when the starter says ''Ready!'' You'll leap out ahead of the others.

Bonus Courses:

Quicksand Valley: Finish first place on the first six runs. Tip: Always take a right at the forks in the road. You'll finish quicker and get points.

Silver Mountain: Finish first at Quicksand Valley.

Ninja Mountain: Finish first at Silver Mountain.

Access Bonus Character Shinobin: Finish first on Ninja Mountain.

All Tracks, Boards, and Character Codes:

All tracks, boards, and hidden characters are accessible from a single screen. To get to that screen, go to the Title screen and punch in: joypad Down, joypad Up, joypad Down, joypad Up. C-Down, C-Up, L, R, Z. Joypad Left, C-Right, joypad Up, B, joypad Right, C-Left, Start. You'll hear confirmation when one of the kids says "Yeah!"

GAME NAME: TWISTED EDGE: EXTREME SNOW-BOARDING

ESRB RATING: E for Everyone. Content suitable for those 6 years or older.

THEME: Extreme snowboarding

PLAYERS: 1 or 2

DEVELOPED BY: Boss Games

PUBLISHED BY: Kemco/Midway

COMMENTS: Call me sentimental or call me a pushover, but there's just something about a video game that offers five difficult settings

with the last one labeled Twisted. This snowboarding game is very similar to 1080°, though
1080° doesn't have that Twisted level. You get
more than 20 basic moves, but the smart player
learns to work them in combos. To earn cheats
you basically have to place high up in the race.

Flower Board: Finish first in all three of the
courses in the first round of competition mode.

Fast Start: Press Up twice on the word "Go!"
at the beginning of the race.

Best Way to Slow: To slow down, bring the
stick down diagonally, either left or right.

RACING AND DRIVING

AUTO RACING

GAME NAME: NASCAR 99

ESRB RATING: E for Everyone. Content suitable for those 6 years or older.

THEME: NASCAR racing

PLAYERS: 1 or 2

DEVELOPED BY: Electronic Arts/EA Sports

COMMENTS: High-speed cars racing down the asphalt. Emotions running red hot. Every mile that passes under the blazing tires might be the last if you don't make a pit stop soon. No, it's not the family vacation. And nobody is going to shout "Don't make me pull this car over!" This is NASCAR racing the way it was meant to be . . . in a video game!

Here you have a choice of 31 drivers and 17 different tracks. Best of all, glamour driver and Winston Cup champ Jeff Gordon in his #24 Chevy. But did you think they were just gonna let you sit behind the wheel as one of NASCAR's legendary speedsters? No way.

You have to earn the privilege, which is half the fun. In order to play as a legend, you have to place in the top five at different tracks. That is, different tracks allow you to play as different drivers.

Tracks include such renowned roadways as Charlotte, Las Vegas, Richmond, and Pocono. Now, here's the drawback of realism. All the tracks, except for Sears Point and Watkins Glen, are oval. Quick, what does that mean? Well, it means that all the turns you're going to make are left-handed. Basically, racing around and around in a circle. Hey, but it's realistic. How realistic is it? Glad you asked. It's so realistic that when you hit the wall, the paint scrapes off the car. It's so realistic that you can read the sponsors' names on the cars. It's so realistic that veteran NASCAR announcers Bob Jenkins and Benny Parsons provide commentary.

The NASCAR 99 starting lineup boasts 31 active drivers. To take the wheel as a NASCAR legend, enter season mode, select 50 percent race length, and place in the top five at specific tracks.

Now, here's the upside to the realism. You have to customize the car to fit the track. Some tracks feature sharp banking turns, such as Bristol, and others have flat-out straightaways, like Indianapolis. Take this customization seriously. Think of it as the coaching part in a football game. The modifications you make to your car will really make a difference in whether you win or lose. For the two-player mode, I'd go so far as to say that the race belongs to the player who can best fine-tune the car and plan a strategy for pit stops.

Short tracks, like Vegas, Texas, and Bristol, usually feature steep banks. That means you have to tinker with the suspension, pushing air over the car, increasing its *wedge*. This will allow you to hang on to those curves better but will reduce your speed. For those tracks with long straightaways, like Indianapolis, Pocono, and Martinsville, you can sacrifice the wedge more.

Also, a word about tire pressure. High pressure in the tires increases speed but wears out the tires faster, and that means more pit stops. (No, not those kinds of pit stops. I know for a fact that drivers go to the bathroom *before* the race begins, and they always go before leaving the house.) Finally, gear ratios can be adjusted either to improve top speed or for a jackrabbit-like acceleration. You have to tinker with this, as well. The twisting and turning tracks, like Atlanta or Sears Point, don't allow for pedal-to-the-metal-type racing. Short bursts of speed and a strategy-type race are your best bets, so you might want low gear ratios, while at tracks with long straightaways, high gear ratios and a higher speed are best.

And, if all this realism wasn't enough, you have your pit crew calling instructions to you over the radio. Listen to them, or you'll be sorry. However, you also have to plan a strategy. Suppose you need fuel but will also need tires soon. Well, you have to make a decision. The best advice is to take care of immediate problems, then go out there and get the kind of lead that buys you time for a later pit stop.

Now, the game features a bunch of different modes and options. For instance, you can complete a full season of 18 races. Eighteen races times 500 laps equals a whole bunch of around and around and around. So, face it, even if you are going almost 200 miles an hour, well, you're still going in a circle. That's probably why the very clever folks who designed the game put in options like Quick Race and Single Race. The Quick Race option chooses a driver and track for you, while the Single Race lets you do the choosing. Personally, I suggest the Single Race mode for learning. This mode will help you get the feel of all the tracks, all the car options, and all the competition. It is, in short, a great practice mode.

There are two modes that I know you won't use, but I'll tell you about them anyway. The first is the Yellow Flag option. When there is an accident ahead, the yellow flags comes out, and all cars form a single rush-hour-type single lane to pass the accident as safely as possible until it is cleared away. You can turn off this option and zip by the accident, but that's dangerous, right? The other option is the Damage option. This is one you'll probably never use either. When this option is activated, it means that your car can break down because of some malfunction or because of damage you've done to it. If you turn this option off, you might be tempted to turn the Indie 500 into the Demolition Derby 500. After all, crashing and smashing a car through 500 laps is fun, isn't it?

Codes:

The secret race car drivers also can be accessed by completing a race in the championship season on the track listed with at least a 50 percent race length and finishing in the top five. However, if you want to access the drivers by code, then you must enter the codes in four seconds or less.

Race as Bobby Allison: Select the Charlotte track and go to the Select Car option. Now comes the speed part. The following code has to be entered in under four seconds. On your mark ... Get set ... Go: C-Up, C-Left, C-Down, C-Right, L, R, L, R, Z, Z. An audio cue will confirm the code and acceptance.

Race as Davey Allison: Select the Talladega track, highlight the Select Car option, and enter the following code in four seconds or less: C-Up, C-Left, C-Down, C-Right, L, R, L, R, L, R. A tone will confirm code entry.

Race as Alan Kulwicki: Select the Bristol track, highlight the Select Car option, and enter the following code in four seconds or less: Z, Z, Z, Z, Z, Z, Z, Z, R, R. A tone will confirm code entry.

Race as Benny Parsons: Select the Richmond track, highlight the Select Car option, and enter the following code in four seconds or less: C-Up, C-Right, C-Down, C-Left, Z, Z, Z, L, Z, Z. A tone will confirm code entry.

Race as Richard Petty: Set the controller configuration to 3. Select the Martinsville track, highlight the Select Car option, and enter the following code in under four seconds: C-Up, C-Up, C-Down, C-Down, C-Left, C-Right, C-Left, C-Right, L, R. A sound will confirm code entry.

Race as Cale Yarborough: Select the Darlington track, highlight the Select Car option, and enter the following code in under four seconds: L, R, L, L, L, R, R, Z. A sound will confirm code entry.

Weird Glitch: Racing in one-player mode and in Dale Jarret's car on the Atlanta track, start a race without qualifying, then after half a lap drive into the exit ramp for the pit. The computer will turn you around, then floor it and you'll see the pit crew floating in the air.

GAME NAME: CRUIS'N WORLD

ESRB RATING: E for Everyone. Content suitable for those 6 years or older

THEME: Global car race

PLAYERS: 1 to 4

DEVELOPED BY: Nintendo/Midway

COMMENTS: Fast cars, exotic places, and weird stunts. Who said you need a license to cruise? The deal with this racer is that it's loaded—*loaded!*—with secret cars, secret tracks, and all kinds of other goodies. To get them you have to either complete the race in a top position or perform a certain number of tricks for bonus points. Remember, the secret to Cruis'n World is a combination of flat-out racing skill and the ability to hot-dog.

Cruis'n World features 15—count 'em, 15—tracks that take game drivers all over the world. Now, we're talking authentic scenery here. According to video legend, the folks at Midway sent the designers out all over the world to take pictures and create authentic tracks.

There are three different difficulty levels: Cruise the World, Championship, and Practice. Hint: Yeah, yeah, yeah, everybody knows what a good driver you are, but don't skip the prac-

tice mode. This is where you earn points to access the secret cars.

The Tracks:

Germany: A relatively easy track that lets you
get the hang of racing. But make no mistake,
this is no baby race, 'cause there are lots of
obstacles and jumps that will send you airborne.
Smart players will take advantage of trick
points earned here to apply toward car up-
grades. Here's a trick: Just before the last ramp
on course, steer left so your car is pointed left,
toward the grassy area. A rock wall will appear.
Steer just to the right of the wall. If you do this
right the car will *automatically* do a flip for
more trick points. The one drawback is that the
wall can be hard to find.

Egypt: A slightly tougher track that Germany.
Watch out for those sharp corners and the soft
sand on the side of the road. Those bored with
pavement driving can use the sand dunes to do
amazing jumps.

Hawaii: Very scenic indeed. Your main challenge here isn't the track but the other drivers.
Here's another shortcut to keep it interesting:
When a scenic overlook sign with red arrow
cones appears in Cruis'n World mode, take a
hard left onto the off-ramp. Trick points are
awarded by this secret.

New York: Narrow streets, aggressive drivers, and a mazelike track. Yep, this is New York City, all right. Just as in real life, think of the rules of the road as more like *suggestions* here. And yes, there are loads of jumps to catch air.

England: Toughest parts of this track are the start and finish when other drivers become a tad too aggressive for safety. New York was good training for the narrow streets.

France: Hey, it's France, so drive as fast as you can and watch out for traffic.

Kenya: Okay, you're in Kenya. *Do not hit the wild animals.* Trust me on this. Avoid the big critters, such as elephants and giraffes, that tend to cross the track at the worst times. So, you didn't trust me, right? Right. And now you're sorry. Listen to me this time: go for the bumps as much as possible to get air and stack up the points.

Italy: Kind of a boring track, but great for going all out. Just don't waste all your juice in mid-course 'cause you're going to need it for the finish.

China: Yeah, yeah, yeah, so you're racing on the Great Wall of China. Did you know it's 1,500 miles long and is the only manmade object visible from space? Just be careful of the crashes that you'll see like clockwork at every lap. Also, be careful getting off the wall and back into the city.

Australia: G'day, mate, and good luck! This is one tough course! You'd think that they'd build better roads down under, but the ones on this track are a mess. Watch for the third bunch of kangaroos to cross the road and then you can get to the hidden road with its super jump.

Mexico: A lot like Australia, but not as tough. Just watch out for the tight turns.

Russia: Another tough mother of a course. The streets are a mess and filled with holes. Use the nitro whenever you can, particularly on the flat streets.

Japan: A cool track filled with tight hairpin turns. Make use of some creative two-wheel driving on this course.

Florida: So, you're back in Florida. Tight turns and swampy land. How'd you get here? You either cruised the whole world or finished in the top three slots in the beginner and pro levels.

The Moon: Brutal competition in reduced gravity. And, as you can imagine, not the best roads in the world. To get to the moon, complete the cruise the world mode under the Easy difficulty level. An animation sequence showing your car being transported to the moon will be displayed; then access the track after the credits roll.

Driving Tricks and Tips:

Barrel Roll: Do a sideways flip by pressing on the gas twice as you turn. Then, and I know this sounds crazy, move the joystick in the opposite direction of the turn. Do this right for bonus points.

Speed Demon Car: Okay, here's the hard part—get at least 9999 points in championship mode to get the car available in the selection screen. It's a lot of work, but it's worth it. The Speed Demon car has a top speed of 230 mph. Here's a tip, though: You can work your way up on bonus points by saving them.

Secret Champ Mode: To get a secret championship mode you have to play like an expert and finish all three Championship courses on beginner and pro levels. The only way to do this is to drive seriously. That means not hitting anything, either on purpose or by accident.

Two-Tone Custom Colors: Really, this particular trick might be more trouble than it's worth. If you're disappointed after all the work, don't blame me. First you have to get at least 150 points in championship mode. Then press L or R on the Car Selection screen.

Turbo Start: Right after the commentator says "Set" press A (gas), A and hold it the second time to get a turbo boost to start the race.

Extra Nitro in Championship Mode: As you begin a race, keep tapping A (the gas) to keep the RPMs running in the red. If you continue to tap, you will start getting the speed effect of a nitro without actually using it. This will help your car get in first place quickly and save your nitro power. To get the most out of the nitro burst, move out of the way of cars in front of you.

Bonus Cars: Begin game play in practice mode and select the Practice Championship option. Finish under the indicated time on the following tracks to unlock the corresponding car. Tip: Not as easy as it looks. The most cautious drivers are rewarded with the cars. Beat the target times in practice mode on the championship courses and the secret cars can be yours.

NY Taxi
LOCATION: Germany
TARGET TIME: 2.27:00

Skool Bus
LOCATION: Egypt
TARGET TIME: 1.07:00

Monsta
LOCATION: Hawaii
TARGET TIME: 3.47:00

Grass Hopper
LOCATION: New York
TARGET TIME: 2.11:00

Bulldog
LOCATION: England
TARGET TIME: 1.46:00

Tommy
LOCATION: France
TARGET TIME: 2.15:00

Conductor
LOCATION: Kenya
TARGET TIME: 2.06:00

Enforcer
LOCATION: China
TARGET TIME: 1.14:00

Surgeon
LOCATION: Australia
TARGET TIME: 1.49:00

Howler
LOCATION: Mexico
TARGET TIME: 1.46:00

Exec
LOCATION: Russia
TARGET TIME: 1.58:00

Rocket
LOCATION: Japan
TARGET TIME: 2.48:00

MORE CAR TRICKS:

Dodge Collisions: The best way to dodge a crash ahead is to activate a turbo boost by pressing A (gas) twice. This will allow you to jump over the crashed car and earn bonus points for the trick.

360° (a complete turn): When your car is at the top of a ramp, press L or R. Easy!

Wheelie: Press A (gas) twice while on a straight road. This also will result in a small boost and a wheelie. It is also a good strategy when you need a boost to catch up. TIP: If you do this when tailgating a car, you can flip.

Side Wheelie: Press A (gas) twice while taking a turn. This is a good strategy for sharp turns.

Flip: Pop a wheelie on a jump by pressing A (gas) twice. You may need to practice this one a little bit. The timing has to be pretty good.

Bonus Tracks: Successfully complete championship mode under the Master Skill difficulty level. You may now access the Russia, Japan, and Florida bonus tracks.

Championship Mode: Finish all three championship courses on Easy, Medium, and Hard difficulty levels to unlock a secret championship mode.

THE BEST OF THE REST: RACING

GAME NAME: **EXTREME G**

ESRB RATING: **T for Teen. Content suitable for those 13 years or older.**

THEME: **Motorcycle racing**

PLAYERS: **1 or 2**

DEVELOPED BY: **Probe**

PUBLISHED BY: **Acclaim**

COMMENTS: A rumble pak is definitely suggested for this motorcycle racing game with 12 different courses.

Codes:

Go to the Vehicle Select screen and press R to get to the Control menu. Highlight the Name option and press the A button. Enter any of the code words that follow for the special powers, then press Start. Don't worry, you won't be racing with a code as a name. There should be a confirmation tone, but this will not change the original name you're playing by. Note: You can repeat this process as many times as you like to really customize your vehicle. To get rid of a special feature you've entered, simply enter it a second time. To get it back, enter it a third time, and to get rid of it again, enter it a fourth time. Well, you get the idea.

Code	Result
NITROID	Unlimited nitros
WIRED	Wire-frame mode
SPIRAL	Spiraling camera angles
PIXIE	No fog mode
NEUTRON	Black and yellow backgrounds
LINEAR	Speeds up the gameplay
XTREME	Increased speed

Code	Result
FERGUS	Shoot some guy named Fergus
FLICK	Speed-blurred effect
2064	Turns bikes into planes
SPYEYE	Overhead camera
XCHARGE	Unlimited lasers and shields
MISTAKE	Unlimited weapons
NOPANEL	No screen display
ANTIGRAV	Upside-down racing
BANANA	Slippery track
GHOSTLY	See-through graphics
FISHEYE	Weird view
UGLYMODE	Another weird view
MAGNIFY	Yet another weird view
STEALTH	And, yes, no view with invisible vehicles

Quitters' mode: Enter ''RA50'' and then start race. At any point during the race, while you are winning, for example, press the Start button and select Quit from the pause menu. The race will end, crediting you with whatever position you happen to be in at the time. For those with absolutely no talent at all for the game, hit Pause before the starting gun in a qualifying race and you'll get the first position.

See the Credits: Win every level in grand prix mode or challenge mode and the option will appear on the main menu.

Race as One of the Game's Programmers: Enter "XGTEAM" as your name. You'll hear a confirmation tone. Go back and enter the programmer's name of your choice. The choices are: ASH, GREG, JOHN, SHAWN, JUSTIN, LLOYD, SIMON, SADIE, GILES. In Practice and Time Trials you'll see the programmer's face on the top of the bike as you race.

Bonus Hawaiian Track: Enter exhibition mode, select Driver Williams, and change his last name to "VACATION." When you return to the Start screen, the new tropical track will be available in the exhibition, time trial and two-player modes.

Cool Tracks and Bikes: "B61GGB5" gives access to all tracks as well as bonus bikes.

GAME NAME: MARIO KART 64
ESRB RATING: E For Everyone. Content suitable for those 6 years or older.
THEME: Cartoon racing

PLAYERS: 1 to 4

DEVELOPED BY: Nintendo

COMMENTS: A racing game with cartoon characters featuring, you guessed it, Mario. Also includes Yoshi, Bowser, and the rest of the Mario gang.

Codes:

To Miss Banana: Press B as you go over a banana and you won't lose control.

Race Reverse Tracks: Come in first and get the Gold Trophies in all four events in the Mario GP 150cc mode, and you get an option where you can race on all 16 courses in reverse.

Mirror Tracks: Win the 150cc Cups and you'll get an option called "extra." After you win the 150cc, reset and the option will be available.

Ghost Option: To get the Course Ghosts option, you must finish the Time Trial runs on these courses at the time indicated or better: Luigi Raceway (1:52:00), Mario Raceway (1:30:00), and Royal Raceway (2:40:00). If you meet or beat the times listed, a Course Ghost will challenge you on your next run. The way to get to the challenge is to select Retry after the race.

Shortcuts:

Koopa Troopa Beach: Just beyond the first ramp, you can turn right around the rocks and head to the sandbar.

Choco Mountain: There is a stone wall just after you go over the hill. As soon as you see it, put your kart in a slide; when you see the end of the wall, jump on it. This may take some practice, but if you get the hang of it, you can jump over the railing and onto the road above you.

Wario Stadium: Go into a power slide just after you get over the big hill and head toward the wall marked by the arrows. Jump the wall to cut into the last part of the track before the finish line.

Rainbow Road: Just before you start flying on the big hill, hop off the course toward the left. You'll fall for a second or two, but be sure to put the brakes on or you'll bounce when you land.

GAME NAME: DIDDY KONG RACING

ESRB RATING: E for Everyone. Content suitable for those 6 years or older.

THEME: Racing

PLAYERS: 1 to 4

DEVELOPED BY: Nintendo

COMMENTS: If you liked, loved, or ever even thought about playing Mario Kart, then you'll like this fantasy racing game. Okay, so the characters are cute, so what? Are you saying you're too *cool* to play cute games? Wanna make something of it, huh? Huh? This game can accommodate up to four players, so if you can't find a guy to play it with you, then get one of your girl cousins or something.

Codes:

Select Game Options on the Start screen, then choose Magic Codes. There will be a space for input, then choose Enter Code. Here are some fun codes to enter after you get to the Magic Codes screen.

All Balloons Are Red: Punch in the word "BOMBSAWAY" and press the Start button. Then select Code List and activate the code. This code will work only in the multiplayer or tracks mode.

All Balloons Turn Green: Punch in "TOXICOF-FENDER" and press the Start button. Then select Code List and activate the code. Again, this code will work only in the multiplayer or tracks mode.

Bananas That Slow You Down: Punch in the word "BOGUSBANANAS" and press the

Start button. Then select Code List and activate the code. This code will work only in the multiplayer or tracks mode. Pay attention; there *are* codes that work in modes other than multiplayer and tracks.

Big Characters and Vehicles: Punch in the word ''ARNOLD'' and press the Start button. Then select Code List and activate the code on the Enter Cheat screen. Remember, just because you've entered the code doesn't mean it will work. You have to activate the code on the Cheat screen first.

Body Armor: Punch in the word ''BODYAR-MOR'' and press the Start button. Then select Code List and activate the code. This code will work only in the multiplayer or tracks mode.

Characters' Voices: Punch in the word ''BLABBERMOUTH'' and press the Start button. Then select Code List and activate the code. This code will work only in the adventure mode.

Full Power-Up: Punch in the word ''FREEFOR-ALL'' and then press Start button. Then select Code List and activate the code. This code will work only in the multiplayer or tracks mode.

Identical Characters: Punch in the word ''DOUBLEVISION'' and press the Start button. Then select Code List and activate the code. This code will work only in the adventure mode.

No Balloons for Race: Punch in the word "BYEBYEBALLOONS." Then select Code List and activate the code. This code will only work in the multiplayer or tracks mode.

No Bananas: Punch in the word "NOYELLOWSTUFF" and press Start button. Then select Code List and activate the code. This code will work only in the multiplayer or tracks mode.

No Zippers: Punch in the word "ZAPTHEZIPPERS" Then select Code List and activate the code. This code will only work in the multiplayer or Tracks mode.

Off-Road Vehicle: Punch in "OFFROAD" and press Start. Then select Code List and activate the code. This code will work only in the multiplayer or tracks mode.

Play as Drumstick: After winning all the trophies and amulets in all stages and tracks of the game, return to the main area and look for the frogs in the swampy part. Check out all the frogs and find the one wearing the wig—or whatever that thing is—and run him over. Drumstick will be available as a playable character after you turn the wig-wearing frog into roadkill.

Play as TT: To play as the TT character, you have to race on all the courses in the time trial mode. Each time you beat the preset track records, you'll earn a little TT icon on the screen. Once you have 20 icons—one for each track— TT will appear as a playable character on the Select screen.

Rocket Fuel Charged: Punch in "ROCKET-FUEL" and press the Start button. Then select Code List and activate the code. This code will work only in the multiplayer or tracks mode.

See Ending Credits: Punch in "WHO-DIDTHIS" and press Start button. Then select Code List and activate the code. This code will work only in the adventure mode.

Small Characters: Punch in "TEENYWEEN-IES" and press the Start button. Then select Code List and activate the code. This code will work only in the adventure mode.

Start with 10 Bananas: Punch in the word "FREEFRUIT" and press the Start button. Then select Code List and activate the code. This code will work only in the multiplayer or tracks mode.

Tracks Modes:

Two-Player Adventure Mode: Punch in the word "JOINTVENTURE" and press the Start button. Then select Code List and activate the code. This code will work only in the adventure mode.

Unbeatable CPU Opponent: Punch in "TIME-TOLOSE" and press the Start button. Then select Code List and activate the code. This code will only work in the multiplayer or tracks mode.

Unlimited Bananas: Punch in the word "VI-TAMINB" and then press the Start button. Then select Code List and activate the code. This code will work only in the multiplayer or tracks mode.

View and Test Music Program: Punch in the word "JUKEBOX" and press the Start button. Then select Code List and activate the code. This code will work only in the adventure mode.

GAME NAME: **F-ZERO X**

ESRB RATING: **E for Everyone. Content suitable for those 6 years or older.**

THEME: **Cyber racing**

PLAYERS: **1 to 4**

DEVELOPED BY: **Nintendo**

COMMENTS: Really weird cyberracing at extreme speeds. I have no idea what the story is all about here, but the graphics are really knockout.

Codes:

Shrinkage: Go to the Vehicle Select screen and hold down the L and R buttons. Then press C-Left and C-Down simultaneously. All vehicles will turn small and then return to normal size after you complete the current circuit.

Color Changes: Go to the Adjust Your Machine screen and press the R button to scroll through the various paint jobs.

View the Machine: Go to the Adjust Your Machine screen and press the C buttons to view your vehicle from different angles.

GAME NAME: **F1 POLE POSITION 64**

ESRB RATING: **E for Everyone. Content suitable for 6 years or older.**

THEME: **Formula-1 racers**

PLAYERS: **1**

DEVELOPED BY: **Human Entertainment**

PUBLISHED BY: **Ubi Soft**

COMMENTS: Yeah, Formula-1 racers! Very realistic, and if you happen to run across a really,

really old person, he might remember a similar arcade game. If he tells you it cost a nickel to play it for an hour, don't listen. The top-of-the-line games cost a whole quarter back then, but kids had to walk ten miles in the snow to a log-cabin mall to play them. Tip: Don't be put off by the controls. There are a lot of them, and they take a little practice.

SECRET CAR: To gain access to the Secret Car, you have to win World Grand Prix in any difficulty level or Damage option you choose. Then save the results to your controller. The next time you restart the game, hold down the A button while on the Title screen. When the Mode screen comes up, you will have a new choice of an F1 car.

GAME NAME: TOP GEAR RALLY

ESRB RATING: E for Everyone. Content suitable for 6 years or older.

THEME: Stock car racing

PLAYERS: 1 or 2

DEVELOPED BY: Boss Games

COMMENTS: A realistic stock car racing game. There's stunning graphics and knockout realistic detail here. But if you get bored with the regulation-style racing, there are also enough goofy codes to keep the game interesting.

Codes:

Open All Tracks (But Not Mirror Tracks): Works in arcade, time attack, and practice modes. Press A, Left, Left, Right, Down, Z after a race begins. Codes may be entered at any time during game play.

All Nine Cars (But Not Bonus Cars): Go to arcade mode. Then punch in: A, Left, Left, C-Down, A, Right, Z.

Mirror Tracks: Right, Left, C-Down, C-Right, C-Down, Z.

Beach Ball Car: When a race starts, punch in: B, B, A, Left, Left, C-Down, A, Right.

Helmet Car: When a race starts, punch in: Up, Up, Z, B, A, Left, Left.

Weird Graphics: When a race starts, punch in B, Left, Right, Up, Left, Z. Since these graphics are so ugly, you may not want to enact this mode. Remember, you have to repeat the code to turn them off.

Rainbow Mode: When a race starts, punch in: C-Down, Z, B, Up, Up, Right. Repeat to return to normal mode.

To See Completion Date: Hold down all four C buttons at once at the Title screen.

Mirror Cars: Access the mirror car mode when a race starts by pressing: Right, Up, Left, C-Down, C-Down, A, Right, Z. Then exit the race and start a new race. When you get to the last screen before the race, press C-Down to change your car to a mirror paint job. This works for all cars.

Drive Ice Cube (Kupra) Car: When a race starts, press: C-Down, Up, B, Right, A, C-Down A, Right.

Drive the Milk Truck: When a race starts, press: Down, A, Right, Z, Right, Up, C-Down.

View Long Version of the Credits: Go to the Main Menu screen and select Options, then highlight Load Configuration. After that enter: C-Down, Right, Down, Z. This offers the full credits rather than the shorter version accessed from the Options Menu screen.

No-Blur: B, Left, Right, Up, Left, Z, Right.

Strip Mine: To get to the Strip Mine, come in at first place on every track during the sixth session.

GAME NAME: **SAN FRANCISCO RUSH: EXTREME RACING**

ESRB RATING: **E for Everyone. Content suitable for those 6 years or older.**

THEME: **City street racing**

PLAYERS: **1 or 2**

DEVELOPED BY: **Atari Games**

COMMENTS: Eight different really fast cars and a city filled with hills. What more is there to say? Oh, yeah, some outstanding special codes, such as racing a car that just happens to be on fire. (Now, how did that happen?)

Codes:

Car Sizing: At the Car Select screen, enter and hold down C-Down and C-Up. Release both, then press and hold C-Up and then C-Down. New car options will appear.

Different Colors of Fog: Hold the Z button down while pressing C-Down three times. The color of the fog should change after the third tap on C-Down.

Drive Upside Down: At the Set-up screen, press: Up, Right, Down, Left, Down, Right, Up, Left.

Exploding Car: Go to the Car Select screen and press: C-Right, C-Right, Z, C-Down, C-Up, Z, C-Left, C-Left.

Exploding Cones: Go to the Set-up Screen and press: Left-Shift, Right-Shift, Left-Shift, Right-Shift.

Night Fog: Go to the Options screen and change Fog to the Heavy setting. Then hold the four C buttons down; there should be a new option, Foggy Night.

Set Your Car on Fire: At the Car Select screen, hold down C-Up and press Z four times. Repeat the process to put the fire out.

Tire Size (back): Go to the Car Select screen and press and hold down C-Right and C-Left. Release them, and then press and hold down C-Left and C-Right. After you release the buttons, you will see codes.

Tire Size (front): Go to the Car Select screen and press and hold down C-Left, then C-Right. Release both buttons. Then press and hold down C-Right, then C-Left. After you release the buttons, you will see the codes.

GAME NAME: **RUSH 2: EXTREME RACING USA**

ESRB RATING: **E for Everyone. Content suitable for those 6 years or older.**

THEME: **Deranged driving game**

PLAYERS: **1 or 2**

DEVELOPED BY: Atari Games

PUBLISHED BY: Midway

COMMENTS: Here's a game where you get to play crash dummy by driving very fast and hitting whatever you want. This pumped-up sequel takes every bad driving habit and incorporates it into a game. You get a choice of 16 different cars, all of them able to do the *air thing,* including a standard sports model and a van. It's a driving game that dares to ask the question: "Are you nuts enough?"

Codes:

To access the cheat menu, go to the Set-Up screen and hold L, R, Z. Now, while still holding them down, press all four of the C buttons. This takes a little practice, and it doesn't hurt if you just happen to have seven fingers on each hand, like a cousin of mine, but it can be done. And, when you do it right, the cheats menu will pop up under the sound option. Now use your cursor to activate the Cheat menu codes:

Auto-Abort: Quickly press C-Up, C-Up, C-Up, C-Up.

Body Size: Hold Z and C-Down and press C-Up, then hold Z and C-Up and press C-Down.

Do the Dew! Soda Car (Mountain Dew Car):
Press L, R, and C-Down; then L, R, and C-Left;
then L, R, and C-Up; then L, R, C-Right, C-
Right; then press Z. (Man, that's a lot of work!
An easier way is to collect the Mountain Dews
floating around. You need to collect all four of
them, though.)

Exploding Cars: Tap Z and C-Up; then C-Right,
C-Down, C-Left, C-Left, C-Left, C-Left, C-
Left, C-Left, C-Up, C-Right, C-Down, C-Left,
C-Left, C-Left, C-Left.

Exploding Cone: Hold Z and tap L, R, R, R, R.

Fog Color: Hold Z and press C-Left, C-Up, C-
Right, C-Down, C-Down, C-Down.

Frame Scale: Hold Z, C-Down, and press C-Up.
Then hold Z, C-Up, and press C-Down.

Game Timer: Hold Z, C-Down, press C-Up,
then hold Z, C-Up, and press C-Down.

High Speed: Hold L and R and press C-Up, C-
Down, C-Left, C-Right.

Inside-Out Car: Hold C-Right and C-Down, and
press L, R, Z.

Invincibility: Press L, C-Up, R, R.

Invisible Car (you just see the wheels): Hold L and R, and press C-Up, C-Down, C-Down, C-Down, C-Down, C-Down.

Invisible Track: Hold L and R, and press C-Down, C-Up, C-Up, C-Up, C-Up, C-Up.

Killer Rats: Hold L and R, and press Z, Z, Z, Z.

Levitation: Hold L, R, Z, and press C-Up, C-Up, C-Up, C-Up.

Massive Mass: Hold L and R and press C-Up, C-Down, C-Left, C-Right.

New York Taxi Cabs: Press R, L, Z, C-Up, C-Down, C-Up.

Resurrect: Hold Z, C-Left, and press C-Right. Then hold Z, C-Right, and press C-Left.

Suicide Mode: Hold Z, and press C-Down, C-Left, C-Up, C-Right, C-Right.

Tire Size: Hold Z and C-Left and press C-Right, then hold Z and C-Right and press C-Left.

How to Earn Cars:

Taxi: Get three keys on any level.

Hot Rod: Get six keys on any level.

Formula-1 Racer: Get nine keys on any level.

GAME NAME: Automobili Lamborghini
ESRB RATING: E for Everyone. Content suitable for those 6 years or older.
THEME: Exotic vehicle racing
PLAYERS: 1 to 4
PUBLISHED BY: Titus
COMMENTS: Here it is, some of the world's most expensive and exotic cars racing along and . . . breaking down. How much more realistic can you get than that? This game features sleek speedsters like Lamborghinis, Porsches, Ferraris, Bugattis, Dodge Vipers, and the super speedy McLaren F1. In addition to the fancy wheels, this game offers six high-performance racing circuits. You definitely want to put the rumble pak on for this one.

TIPS AND STRATEGIES:

The tracks have a lot of shortcuts, but you have to search them out. The best way is to turn around and drive the course backward. This way you don't have a time limit and can explore the terrain at your own pace.

Drive a Fancy Pants Car: The fancy cars are awarded for finishing first. The more times you finish a course, the more cars you get.

Novice Level
    Arcade: Basic Series—Porsche
    Arcade: Pro Series—Ferrari
    Normal Championship Series—
        Bugatti

Expert Level
    Arcade: Basic Series—Ferrari
    Arcade: Pro Series—Dodge Viper
    Normal Championship Series—
        McLaren (and accesses reverse
        tracks)

Reverse Tracks: To race on reverse tracks you have to beat the championship mode in novice and expert.

Fast Start and Burning Rubber: Hit the gas as soon as the announcer gets done saying "One!" The timing has to be just right. It takes awhile to get the hang of this trick.

GAME NAME: GT 64 CHAMPIONSHIP EDITION

ESRB RATING: E for Everyone. Content suitable for those 6 years or older.

THEME: International auto racing

PLAYERS: 1 or 2

DEVELOPED BY: Imagineer

PUBLISHED BY: Ocean

COMMENTS: A pretty standard racer here with a choice of 14 cars, including Acura's NSX and

Toyota's Supra-GT. This is track racing on an international level so you move around the world on six circuits, from Japan to the United States, with each track offering its own set of challenges. The one standout feature players will like is the ability to customize the cars down to gear ratios. And then, of course, there are those tricky weather changes. You can race in a championship mode for the full international circuit or a single race in Time Trial, where you adjust the number of laps. There aren't a lot of tricks and codes here. The game's best feature is its realism. This is a solid racer with enough realism to keep enthusiasts playing.

Tips:

Fast Start: Jam down on the gas at the yellow starting light.

Reverse Track: Win the championship on the Easy level.

GAME NAME: **OFF ROAD CHALLENGE**

ESRB RATING: **E for Everyone. Content suitable for those 6 years or older.**

THEME: **Off-road racing**

PLAYERS: **1 or 2**

PUBLISHED BY: **Midway**

COMMENTS: Remember this beauty from the arcade? This is a four-wheeling racing game with some very interesting tracks. Don't miss Area 51!

Codes:

Go to the Vehicle Select screen and press the following buttons to display some hidden vehicles.

The Crusher: C-Right.

Toyota 4x4 Monster: C-Up.

Thunder Bolt: C-Left.

The Punisher: C-Down.

To access hidden tracks, go to the Track Select screen first.

Flagstaff: Hold down L and punch in left on the joypad. You'll hear a confirmation tone. Then highlight the Mojave course on Select screen and hold the Z button while pressing A.

Guadalupe: Hold down R and hit down on the joypad. You'll hear a confirmation tone. Highlight the Las Vegas course and hold the Z button while pressing A.

El Cajon: Hold L and R and hit up on the joypad. You'll hear a confirmation tone. Highlight the El Paso course, hold the Z button, and press A.

AIR AND WATER RACING

GAME NAME: WAVE RACE 64

ESRB RATING: E for Everyone. Content suitable for those 6 years or older.

THEME: Jet ski racing

PLAYERS: 1 or 2

DEVELOPED BY: Nintendo

COMMENTS: Wave Race is one of the all-time great games for the N64 system. And I'll tell you why. It's not because the graphics are great (although they are) or the theme is outstanding (Jet Skis). It's great because it's one of the few games out there easy enough for parents to play.

So, this is a game you can play with your parents. Even better, with the few simple tricks I'm going to tell you about, you can kick their butts. Hey, what's better than that?

You can compete against the CPU or another player for speed or stunts. You have a choice of four riders, each with different amounts of grip, handling, acceleration, top speed, and collision stability. Also, you can customize each rider's Jet Ski. The game also features eight different courses. The courses start off easy, with the mild and warm Dolphin Park, and progress through the frozen Glacier Coast. However, you have to earn your way to other courses, winning in Hard, Expert, and Reverse levels in the championship modes.

You don't have to be a rocket scientist to figure out that you need more stability and grip when competing on the stunt mode. That's easy. But listen: You should familiarize yourself with all four riders, using them to compete against the CPU. This will give you an advantage when competing against friends.

Tips:

To get off to a flying start at the beginning of a race, jam down on the accelerator button as soon as the announcer shouts ''Go!'' Okay, this takes a little practice, but when competing against a second player, it can give you a real advantage.

In order to reduce the waves and effects of the ramps, press B before hitting a wave or ramp. Your air time will be cut by a lot.

After taking a spill into the water, keep tapping the A button. You'll get up and going on your Jet Ski a lot faster.

Cheat:

Okay, suppose you stink at the stunt stuff. It happens, don't feel bad. Or suppose you share the game with someone—a brother or sister, for instance—and want to show off big scores in the stunt mode. This trick will help. Well, it won't do the stunts for you, but it will give you sky-high points for doing them.

Just after you hit the water, press Start to pause the game. This might take some practice, because your timing has to be just right. Use the announcer's voice to cue you. As soon as he starts talking, hit the button. If you did it correctly, the announcer will keep talking, but the game will give you a ton of extra points.

Why does this happen? Who knows? Who cares? After you complete the course, check out all the points you got for pretty easy tricks.

Marine Fortress (works only on hard, expert, reverse modes): When you complete the course once, a steel door will open as you come close to it. Going through the door leads to the short-cut.

Port Blue (works on hard mode): Always go through the tunnel on the right.

Twilight City (works only on hard and expert modes): Jump over the ramp at the beginning of the race. If you try it on expert mode, jump the ramp and then go under the wall.

Southern Island (works for normal, hard, and expert modes): Going under the pier saves some time. Dive under it for the first lap, then on the second lap you'll be able to ride under it.

Ride the Dolphin: This trick allows you to ride a dolphin in the warm-up mode. To do it, select Dolphin Park in stunt mode. For this to work, you have to go through all the rings and complete all of the stunts, including handstand, spin, stand and somersault, barrel roll left off a ramp, barrel roll right off a ramp, flip off a ramp, dive underwater from a ramp, and so on. It isn't easy. You have to get a strategy down that best fits you. I've found that doing as many tricks as I can before the ramps start helps. Once the ramps start, you'll be pressed for time and distracted. It may take a few attempts, but it's worth it. If you did it all correctly, the dolphin will speak to you in dolphin language when you cross the finish line. That squeaking is the signal that he's available for riding.

Now, go back to the menu and choose championship mode and normal skill. Also, pick the Warm-up option. Then choose your craft by holding down the stick and pressing A. When you go back to the water, you'll be on a dolphin.

Hey, when you go back into the demo/attack

mode, you'll see people riding dolphins.

To see the baby dolphins, go into championship mode, normal and warm-up. Do everything the dolphin does, following him around the track three times. On the third lap the dolphin should jump the bridge and the babies will appear.

THE BEST OF THE REST: AIR AND WATER RACING

GAME NAME: **AERO GAUGE**

ESRB RATING: **E for Everyone. Content suitable for those 6 years or older.**

THEME: **Hovercraft racing**

PLAYERS: **1 or 2**

DEVELOPED BY: **Locomotive**

PUBLISHED BY: **ASCII Entertainment Software**

COMMENTS: This is a high-speed game. You get a choice of five hovercrafts to start out with; more choices are offered by posting a track time ending in 64 . . . get it? N64, Nintendo 64, track time of 64. Good, I knew you would. Hey, but how about this? One of the weird hidden racers looks like an N64 controller. Another thing that's cool is that you have a choice of more than 20 sound tracks. Kind of like picking music for your own action-adventure movie. However, that's the only glitz and glam here. This isn't a complicated game. Speed is the big thing in this stripped-down racing video.

Codes and Strategies:

Fast Start: Press down both A and B buttons. When the starter shouts "GO!" or just a little before, let go of the B button. Your craft will get a faster start.

Speed Boost: During a race hold down the A and Z buttons, then bring the joystick down hard (left or right, it doesn't matter) and quickly press A. The timing has to be just right on this code, but it does work.

Access Hidden Crafts and Codes: You have to do this trick carefully, and it requires two controllers. When you turn the game on, press Start on the first controller. You should see the screen that reads Push Start. Then on the second controller press up on the joypad, C-Down, R, L, and Z all at the same time. Release them, and quickly press either Start or the A button on the first controller. This should take you to the Grand Prix level and give you access to some nifty stuff.

Bonus Cars:

Drive the Controller: To drive a Nintendo controller, finish the game in any time that ends with 064.

Vengeance: Finish in first place on Expert setting, driving the Avenger.

Reaper: Finish in first place on Expert level, driving Shredder.

Dominator: Finish in first place on Expert level, driving the Black Lightning.

GAME NAME: PILOTWINGS 64

ESRB RATING: E for Everyone. Content suitable for those 6 years or older.

THEME: Aircraft racing

PLAYERS: 1

DEVELOPED BY: Nintendo/Paradigm Simulation

COMMENTS: This is a game you have to play alone; after all, it's lonely up there. You get a choice of craft and the ability to shoot. If you don't take your flight simulator too seriously, this is a great game.

Codes:

Day to Night: Go to the Beginner level and find the cave in front of the chapel on a hill. You'll see a stream of water coming out of the cave. Follow the water inside to the sewer. The game will pause, then start again. When you leave the cave it will be night.

Shoot Mario: When you get to Mount Rushmore and see the giant Mario face, shoot it with gyro missiles. If you make a direct hit, the face will change to Mario's enemy, Wario.

Easy Birdman Stage: Fly under the bridge on the first level and get the star.

Fuel: Any gas station will give you fuel. The gas station in Little States gives you unlimited fuel for free. Go to the gas station at a road junction in the southeast, between the space shuttle pad in Florida and the Mississippi River in Georgia. Land in the parking lot, between the sign and the building. Now, go to the center line and your fuel tank will get filled. However, if you stop while in the copter, then the level will end.

N.Y. to S.F. in Nothing Flat: In the Little States level, start in New York and find the building with the open door just west of the park. Go inside, walk past the N64 sign, and enter the next door. You'll be in San Francisco.

ADVENTURE RPG, PUZZLES, AND OTHER GAMES

ADVENTURE RPG

GAME NAME: THE LEGEND OF ZELDA: OCARINA OF TIME

ESRB RATING: E for Everyone. Content suitable for those 6 years or older.

THEME: Quest role-playing game

PLAYERS: 1

DEVELOPED BY: Nintendo

COMMENTS: If you haven't heard or played Nintendo's latest installment of Zelda yet, well, I can't help you. The game itself was an event when it was introduced. Hailed as the pinnacle of role-playing games (RPGs), The Legend of Zelda: Ocarina of Time is the game that all the others have to beat. It contains a *huge* fantasy world in which you can interact and play with almost everything. Hey, the game takes place within two full days in the mythical world, with game play simulating nighttime and daytime and everything in between. And there are also a bunch of very cool time travel tricks. Link actually grows up in the game. There are stunning graphics and a load of minigames to play along the way.

Okay, so if you're not familiar with the Zelda, here's the deal. I'm giving you this as a very basic overview, so Zelda fans don't get mad at me.

You play the role of Link, a young elven (that's a boy elf, for those not familiar with the word) living in the land of Hyrule. After having a nightmare about the bad guy Ganondorf, he starts his quest/adventure. The game eventually turns into a rescue mission of the Princess Zelda. On the quest you travel through deserts, a volcano, forests, and dungeons in the Kingdom of Hyrule. So basically, while on your quest you run around beating up baddies, playing minigames, and hunting out clues. You explore the world created for you. If you're one of those people who just likes to get to the end of a game fast, then forget it, RPGs aren't for you. In the world of RPGs, the adventure of exploring the mythical world is the game. They say that Zelda can be completed in 40 hours. I don't believe it. For one thing, just playing and enjoying all the minigames, like the shooting gallery, the fishing game, and horseback riding, can take you 40 hours. For another thing, this is a world you really want to explore.

The ocarina in the title is the magical flute. Within the game there are 12 songs that you can play on the flute. Six of them provide Link with magical powers, and the last six give him the ability to warp around the world. The catch, of course, is that he/you has to learn to play the songs from a character in the game. Don't worry about remembering the songs, the system saves them for you. However, you might want to experiment a little, too. For instance, a friend of mine started playing Beatles' songs on the ocarina.

Unlike other video games, you really don't want to know everything there is to know about the adventure: knowing all the strategies and cheats diminishes the fun. Think of it as a movie where you don't want people telling you the ending. With that in mind, I've included some of my favorite tricks. I hope they won't ruin this outstanding game for you.

Strategy:

Spend time at the beginning in Kokiri village. This is the closest thing to a practice or training ground in the game. The various tasks you do will teach you all the controller functions, plus you'll get valuable rupees. What a deal!

Don't shop till you drop. A lot of the items you need don't have to be purchased. So hang on to your rupees. For instance, you can catch a fish for a lot less than buying one. And remember, there are no credit cards or ATMs in the Kingdom of Hyrule.

Link can interact with a huge number of

things in the game, so don't get so tied up about winning that you don't explore properly. Interact with as many things in as many ways as you can. Go ahead, chop down signs, break things, and overall just act like you have a bad attitude.

The easiest way to break open crates is to roll into them. You do this by pressing Forward A.

The game features a lock-on mode. That is, when Link recognizes an enemy or an object he has to deal with, you press the Z button. Use this feature a lot. It's a big help and allows for special moves. When in this mode you can side-step and circle Link's enemies. The Z button, which positions the camera, is also useful when locked in rooms, such as dungeons, to help find a way out.

When in doubt, press the B button. During regular play when nothing special is happening, this button controls jumping. In special situations, as when faced with a ladder or a wall, the B button controls special movements.

Remember, there is no jump button. Just run or walk toward the object you want to jump over or across and Link automatically jumps. You have to trust the game to make this move for you. Actually, it's one less thing to think about and comes in pretty handy.

Play with the sound up so you can hear the Skulltula coins. They make a scratching kind of sound. If you hear one but don't see one, look up. Chances are it's above Link's head.

Talk to strangers at every opportunity. Even the most unlikely person can have a valuable clue.

If you are low on life force, choose to avoid battle. Not all battles help progress you through the game. However, it is important to fight once Link enters the dungeon territory.

Because time changes during the game from day to night and then day again, you have to plan your strategy around the time. For instance, things are closed at night and might not allow you to enter. The thing to remember is that Hyrule Castle closes at around dusk. If you are outside at night, be prepared to encounter some monsters.

Tricks:

Attack of the Killer Chickens: Attack a chicken with your sword and a whole herd (or is it flock?) of chickens will descend on you. Don't bother fighting them, though, just run. Don't worry, they won't follow you through the entire game. There is another use for the chickens— I know, I know, they're really called *cuccos*. But they *taste* like chicken. If you find one near a ledge or fall, you can pick it up and use it as a glider.

Break It, Fix It: If you get mad and smash a sign (hey, these things happen), you can put it back together again by playing "Zelda's Lullaby" on the flute.

Free Milk: If you play "Epona's Song" on the flute next to a cow, the cow will fill your bottle up for free. However, you do need a bottle. And remember, Lon Lon milk replenishes Link's life meter.

GAME NAME: **SUPER MARIO 64**

ESRB RATING: **E for Everyone. Content suitable for those 6 years or older.**

THEME: **Role-playing adventure**

PLAYERS: **1**

DEVELOPED BY: **Nintendo**

COMMENTS: In case you didn't know, this is the game that made the N64 system great. It's a 3-D adventure starring the familiar character Mario. And everyone knows Mario. He started life as a 2-D character in Donkey Kong but quickly became a star. The plumber from Brooklyn made it big-time.

If you have the N64, you've probably played the game. This is the kind of game that your six-year-old cousin who eats paste can play and enjoy. That's not to say it's easy, but it's very cool to run the little guy around.

To briefly review, Mario shows up at Princess Toadstool's castle and finds that she's been kidnapped by the evil Bowser, who is king of the Koopas. Bowser also has hung all these weird paintings on the wall that Mario can jump into and reach really weird worlds. Anyway, in order to defeat Bowser, Mario has to collect at least 70 Power Stars and then fight the guy three times.

What? You say that doesn't make sense? Who cares? And who asked you, anyway? Just go back to reading about the game!

Super Mario 64 has 15 levels (plus two bonus levels) and each level has six courses. On each course there are seven Power Stars. Got it? That's 105 Power Stars. There are also 15 more Power Stars hidden around the castle, for a grand total of 120. In the course of his adventure, Mario has to face and fight Bowser three times. As you collect Power Stars, you can gain entrance into more parts of the castle and collect more stars. So, to open the doors marked with Power Stars, you have to collect the number of stars the door indicates.

In the old game Mario could just run around. It was pretty good, but nothing special. In this new game, he can punch and kick, do fighting combos, fly, swim, climb, do a running long jump, somersault, bounce off walls, bounce on his butt, crawl, and back flip. He can't do all of these all the time, but his added movements are great. He can even tiptoe.

Now, I'm not going to tell you everything you need to know to win the game and become the hero of the world and boss of all your friends. Not only would that not be fair, but it wouldn't be a lot of fun. Most of the fun in Super Mario is exploring the castle. But let's face it, everyone needs some help every once in a while, so here are some tips and strategies for completing the game once you've gotten pretty far into it. Also, there are lots of cool things to do even after you have 120 Power Stars.

The Regular Levels

Course 1: Bob-omb Battlefield	Course 9: Dire, Dire Docks
Course 2: Whomp's Fortress	Course 10: Snowman's Land
Course 3: Jolly Roger Bay	Course 11: Wet-Dry World
Course 4: Cool, Cool Mountain	Course 12: Tall, Tall Mountain
Course 5: Big Boo's Haunt	Course 13: Tiny-Huge Island
Course 6: Hazy Maze Cave	Course 14: Tick Tock Clock
Course 7: Lethal Lava Land	Course 15: Rainbow Ride
Course 8: Shifting Sand Land	

Bonus Levels:

The Princess's Secret Slide: You need one Power Star to enter the Secret Slide. The slide is on the castle's first floor on the right side with a star on the door. It's a small room with a big slide. To get to the slide, jump at the window. If you can get to the bottom of the slide you automatically get a Power Star. However, if you can get to the bottom of the slide fast, then you get two Power Stars. How fast? Less than 21 seconds. To get to the bottom of the slide fast, go down it headfirst and hold the joystick in the forward position.

Secret Aquarium: You need a minimum of three Power Stars to enter the level. At Jolly Rancher Bay, look up and there will be a black square. Go in the square and you will be in the aquarium. The idea here is to have Mario swim and collect coins. After you have all eight of the Red Coins, then the Power Star will show up.

Mario Over the Rainbow: The third and final secret level is Mario Over the Rainbow and you need 50—count 'em, 50!—Power Stars to enter. This level is on the third floor of the castle. It's kinda tough to find, so I'll tell you. It's the opening to the left of the clock. You have to find eight coins here. Seven of them you get by flying around, but to get the eighth, you have to shoot Mario from a cannon and land on it.

Strategy:

Where You Fight Bowser: The first time you fight Bowser is in a level called Dark World. This course is located through the Big Star

Door on the castle's ground floor. To kill the critter, you have to have Mario run up behind him and grab his tail. Use the pad to spin him around, then press B to send him flying. Now, here's the thing: You have to throw him into one of the bombs or he won't die. (But you knew that already, didn't you?) After you've made turtle soap from Bowser, walk over to him and get a Big Key. This key will open the lower floor of the castle.

The second time you meet Bowser it's in the Fire Sea on the lower floor of the castle. The Big Star door down there will open into the area. Again, grab him by the tail, but be careful. Get him just after he gets tired out from running. And again, throw him into a bomb. After you've blown him up for a second time (no big deal, right?), get another key from him.

The third time you run into the Bowser—doesn't this guy ever learn?—he's on the top floor of the castle. The battle, naturally, is called Bowser in the Sky. And again, you reach him by going through a Big Star door on the third floor. (Note: If you don't have at least 70 Power Stars, then the stairs will go on forever. There are kids out there who have been waiting six, eight, and even nine months for Mario to reach the end of the stairs. The key you get from Bowser will unlock the door and get you on to the stairs, but unless you have enough Power Stars, it's a waste of time to even start on them.)

To defeat Bowser for the last time, you have to make him laugh until milk comes out his nose. Okay, I was kidding. Relax, it was a joke. This time you have to grab Bowser by the tail and throw him into the bombs *three times*.

When Bowser blows up the last time, walk over to him and get a jumbo star. Just touch the star and you've won the game.

Tip:

To prevent Mario from getting hurt when falling from a cliff, do a butt-stomp. This will prevent him from suffering serious damage.

There's a lot going on in Mario's world. It's easy to lose count of how many Power Stars you have at any given time. To get an accurate count, put the game on Pause, then press up or down to check out the places in the castle you've been. Each level will include a kind of visual count. A filled-in white Power Star means you've collected that star, but a clear one means you've missed something. If Power Stars don't appear with a coin total for the level, you either have not collected the full 100 coins or didn't get the Power Star.

Dropping in on Yoshi: After you've collected 120 Power Stars, go back outside and you'll see a cannon. Shoot yourself up to the roof of the castle and you'll find—guess who?—Yoshi! Have a chat with him and he'll hand over 100 extra lives. Who knows, they could come in handy.

A Dangerous Man with a Hat: In Snowman's Land you can use your cap as a weapon! The way to do this is to go to the Snowman and get your cap blown off. Now, just a little to the left is a tree that is also a teleport. Get teleported to another tree and then teleported back. When you return to the original spot where your cap was blown off, there will be two caps, one of which you can use as a weapon. Be careful, though, because Mario gets more damage done to him when he's hit without his cap. You can do this trick a lot of times and get a bunch of caps. Unfortunately, you get to keep the extra cap only as long as you're on that level. And because Mario should never be without his cap, make sure he doesn't lose it. There are only three places where he can misplace the famous cap: Shifting Sand Land, Snowman Land, and Tall, Tall Mountain.

On Level 3 in Jolly Roger Bay you'll find the Eel around the Power Stars keys you need. Then in Level 8 you'll find the Big Bird. Stay away from these guys as much as possible. You can't beat them. And don't let that bird steal your cap. Remember, without a cap Mario gets hurt more easily. If the bird does manage to get the cap, then fight him for it.

When you have at least 50 Power Stars, head downstairs to the basement near Levels 6 and

8. There you'll find a yellow rabbit (who knew?). Catch the rabbit by grabbing for him. The best way is to wait until it tries to run past you, then reach out and touch it. The rabbit will ask to be let go. Let it go and get a Power Star. Then catch it again and get a second Power Star.

Tricks:

Camera Angling: After you defeat Bowser for the final time, make certain you have another controller plugged into the game. You can use this second controller's pad to change camera angles for the final scene and the credits. It's pretty cool.

Doorway Weirdness: When you go through a door on certain levels, very strange things will happen if you turn back quickly and try to go back through it.

Mama Penguin Trick: Bring the baby penguin back to its mother, but instead of taking the Power Star from her, grab the baby back and she'll chase you. Now, if you really want to be mean, throw the baby penguin over the side of the cliff and the mother will jump after it.

Messing with Mario's Face: When Mario's face appears on the title screen, hold down the A button. You can pull his nose and mustache by doing this.

GAME NAME: MARIO PARTY

ESRB RATING: E for Everyone. Content suitable for those 6 years or older.

THEME: Mario board game

PLAYERS: 1 to 4

DEVELOPED BY: Hudson Soft

PUBLISHED BY: Nintendo

COMMENTS: Mario Party is one of those games that will leave players asking themselves "Why didn't someone think of that before?" If you don't already know by now, Mario Party is a video "board game" where one to four players can compete as their favorite Mario characters. These include Mario, Luigi, Peach, Yoshi, Wario, and Donkey Kong. So, Mario Party is also kind of a family reunion that traces Mario from his earliest days in video game fame.

This is a board game where the board is animated. A very cool idea, indeed.

One of the really cool features is the ability to set the number of turns a game lasts. So, a bunch of people can pick a 20-, 40-, or 60-turn game.

Of course, there's a hitch. Like all board games, Mario Party is the most fun when playing with friends. Playing alone is like, well, playing a board game alone. And, as we all know, playing a board game alone is about as much fun as smelling the socks you left under the bed last week. The other thing to remember is, because you're rolling dice to see how many turns you take around one of six different boards (and two secret boards), well, you don't get that much better with practice. This is a game where there's a lot of luck involved, so the competition really isn't the same as with a standard video game. The other good thing about this game is that even if you happen to be playing against someone who isn't that good at regular video games, the Party is still fun.

The six boards included are: Donkey's Jungle Adventure, Peach's Birthday Cake, Yoshi's Tropical Island, Wario's Battle Canyon, Luigi's Engine Room, and, of course, Mario's Rainbow Castle.

The one spot in the game where you might get better with practice is with the mini-games included in Mario Party. In all there are 56 of the mini-games included in the game play. The mini-games are simple, but fun. Sometimes you're playing against another player and sometimes you're playing against two or three others. And sometimes up to four players are battling the CPU. For instance, in one mini-game all the players get on top of giant balls and try to knock each other off. Another mini-game is a kind of sled race. And still another is a video game version of "Simon Says."

The one spot in Mario Party where you can practice is the mini-game house mode, where you can play just the mini-games. Frankly, though, most experienced gamers won't need much practice on the little games, and it's fun to play them with friends. However, you can also "buy" some pretty neat stuff in the shop that can help you in the games. So, the Game House is definitely worth a visit.

The whole point of the game is to collect coins and stars and play the mini-games. When the game ends, the machine rates the players according to their game play and awards more stars. The player with the most stars wins. Ta-da!

Hidden Mini-games:

Bumper Ball Maze 1: To play this game, you have to get to Mini-Game Island and beat Toad in Slot Car Derby.

Bumper Ball Maze 2: Win all 50 minigames on Mini-Game Island and Toad will give you directions.

Bumper Ball Maze 3: Set new records on Bumper Ball Maze 1 and Bumper Ball Maze 2.

Cheat:

To fill the Mushroom Bank, switch to real players from CPU in the last round. This is done easily by pausing, then going to option menu. Once you complete the board game, the players will get to keep all the mushrooms the machine earned during the game.

Bonus Level:

Bowser's Magma Mountain: To get to Bowser's Magma Mountain, you need to earn 1,000 coins. Then you can buy yourself into the extra stage by going to shop and buying the key.

GAME NAME: BANJO-KAZOOIE

ESRB RATING: E for Everyone. Content suitable for those 6 years or older.

THEME: 3-D cartoon adventure

PLAYERS: 1

DEVELOPED BY: Rare/Nintendo

COMMENTS: A bear and a chicken out to stop an evil witch with the help of a mole. Hey, it doesn't get much better than this!

Okay, here's the deal. The ugly witch Gruntilda has kidnapped Banjo's (the bear's) sister Tooty. Why? Because Tooty is pretty and Gruntilda is looking to swap looks with her. A good enough reason as any for a witch in a video game. Banjo and his wise-cracking but helpful sidekick Kazooie the Chicken (okay, Red-Crested Breegull, but he *tastes* like chicken) must rescue Tooty before she becomes a wart-riddled bear. However, they are not alone. Bottles, the mole, helps them out with clues and puzzles.

The game is similar to Mario 64. You have to work your way through a maze and collect items along the way in order to rescue Tooty. In all, there are more than 1,000 different items, such as musical notes, honeycombs, flight pads, golden banjos, and, of course, running shoes and wading boots.

There are 12 different levels, including a Honeycomb level in the beginning that serves as a trainer to practice moves and get the hang of the Banjo-Kazooie teamwork needed to complete the adventure. Then at the end there is a bonus round with secret codes. I know, I know, these are really part of the game, but they still count as codes in my book.

Basic Moves:

There are the usual assortment of moves in Banjo, like walk, jump, punch, duck, and others. The tricky part is picking up more moves as you progress through the game. Along the way to rescue Tooty, you have to learn more moves. When you come across a molehill, be sure to press B. Bottles will pop up and teach you another move, usually a combo.

Kazooie's Killer Cool Moves:

Beak Buster: Kazooie is good on the attack with this move. Simply press A (for a jump) and Z (for the attack) and the bird flies down, beak first, with a lot power. Good for busting up obstacles and opening secrets.

Beak Barge: Z (for beak first) and B (for running) sends the chicken running at an object like an arrow, pointy end first.

Wonder Wings: In this defensive move, Kazooie spreads wings to protect against attacks. But you need Gold Feathers to pull it off. Hold the Z button down, then press the C-Right button for the Wonder Wings.

Tips:

Banjo's Home on Spiral Mountain: Be sure to find all the molehills for Bottles' instructions in the basic strategies such as camera control, swimming, climbing, and so on.

Break the Click Clock Wood Boulder: So, you've gotten near the end of the game and still can't break the rock blocking the beaver hole in the Click Clock Wood. You just need to practice this trick. Get yourself up on the ledge over the rock. Now, start dropping eggs to the right side of the rock. You can swim into the hole on this level, but don't be surprised if the beaver is still asking you to move the rock. Hey, beavers ain't that smart.

Bubble Gloop Swamp: It's best to go over Mumbo's hut, up on the wall, and down the other side. This will save you a lot of time.

Clanker's Cavern: Look inside Clanker's air hole for the Witch Switch. Who'd think of looking there? And remember, you can get in through the air hole as well as through his teeth or gills.

Click Clock Wood: Chickens (okay, Breegulls) can fly, right? Well, Kazoozie can't fly that well in the springtime forest, so turn Banjo into a bee and you can·avoid all kinds of nasty plants and get to the hive. But you can't be a bee in winter; that's when you should depend on Kazooie's Wonder Wing. The wing move is also good in the beehive.

Extra Lives in Mr. Vile's Games: Mumbo can help you turn into an alligator in the Bubble-gloop Swamp. Then enter through the nose of the giant alligator statue and beat Mr. Vile's games to get a puzzle piece. Okay, now here's the tricky part. Leave and reenter to beat Mr. Vile in three games to earn extra lives. However, if you lose any of the games, you will lose a life.

Faster Dialogue: Hold B to scroll the text dialogue faster.

Freezey Peak: See that key in Wozza's Cave? Well, you can't have it. Don't even try. Don't even think about it, okay? Oh, yeah, the Witch Switch is under the snowman. . . . No, not the big snowman, the other one!

Gettin' Grunty: Once you've rescued Tooty, then the game is over, right? Wrong. Go to the party hosted by Mumbo and then back to the furnace. Now it's time to get Grunty herself. After you've stocked up on Gold Feathers, Red Feathers, and Blue Eggs, then head upstairs to the roof. Now be careful, 'cause Grunty is flying her broomstick. Now it's time to kick some witch butt!

Gobi's Valley: So, now you're in the desert and what do you need? Wading boots, naturally. Get them before you enter the desert. The boots are excellent protection from the hot sand. Don't worry, though; if you're smart you won't look like an idiot wearing boots in the desert for long, 'cause you need to get into a pair of running shoes fast! Note: Running shoes and wading boots are available at several locations throughout the valley, but it's best to get the boots before entering. The first pair is in a side chamber.

Grunty's Furnace Fun Fest: This is it, the last level, and it's tough. It's horrible. It's a . . . game-show world. The key to these games is remembering your experiences in the previous nine levels, particularly whatever Grunty's sister, Brentilda, told you about her.

Help from Trash: Get on top of Banjo's house by hopping off the trash can and flying up. When you get on top of the chimney, jump and touch the golden statue of Banjo.

Hint: It's okay to break all the lighted windows in the mansion. In fact, it's really good if you ever want to get out of this level.

Jump Farther: During any jump, press Attack.

Less Damaging Fall: To take less damage from a fall, press Z just before you land.

Mad Monster Mansion Madness: Gotta watch out for ghosts in this level. Best way to fight them is with Gold Feathers. However, lacking Gold Feathers . . . well, RUN! And yes, you can outrun these critters.

Mumbo's Mountain: Smash the huts and you'll find the Musical Notes. Remember, each world has 100 notes that must be collected.

Rusty Bucket Bay: Boom Boxes are a danger on this level. They explode without ever being touched. Kazooie can outrun, er, swim them. Also, spend as much time out of the water as possible. Climb ladders, boxes, whatever you can find to dry out; otherwise the polluted water will soak up all your air. Pay attention to the ship's portholes. Look for the ones that are a little darker than the others and peck them out to discover some valuable notes. There are three such windows.

Skip Dialogue: Press L, R, B to skip the dialogue display.

Slappa and Gobi: Two adversaries are Slappa (a kind of desert worm) and Gobi, the camel. Beak Busters are good against both. Hint: Slappa is best hit when he's down on the ground. Don't attack Gobi directly, just free him from the stone he's chained to.

Treasure Trove Cove: Don't even think about going to Shark's Food Island. There's nothing there of any worth. Also, when you hear the shark music, have Kazooie swim away from the danger. Banjo cannot outswim the shark.

Cheat Codes:

To make these codes work, you have to play all the way up to Treasure Trove Cove and *not* transform at Mumbo's Hut. Then collect the jigsaw pieces from the Underwater Castle in Treasure Trove Cove. Now use the Beak Buster to enter the word "CHEAT" on the floor tiles. *Remember to enter the phrases with no spacing between words*. For instance: "BANJO BEGS FOR PLENTY OF EGGS" becomes: "BANJOBEGSFORPLENTYOFEGGS." Got it? Good, 'cause it ain't that hard to remember. Also remember to spell carefully. If you make a mistake you have to start again, from the outside.

Code	What It Does
A GOLDEN GLOW TO PROTECT BANJO	Infinite Gold Feathers
AN ENERGY BAR TO GET YOU FAR	Max lifebar (8)
BANJO BEGS FOR PLENTY OF EGGS	Infinite eggs
DON'T BE A DUMBO GO SEE MUMBO	99 Mumbo Tokens
GIVE THE BEAR LOTS OF AIR	Infinite air (for swimming)
LOTS OF GOES WITH MANY BANJOS	Infinite lives
NOW YOU CAN FLY HIGH IN THE SKY	Infinite Red Feathers

So, Now That You've Won the Game: To do these tricks you have to complete the game. Is it worth it? Heck, no! But if you finished the darned thing, then you might as well take advantage of these tricks.

Go to Banjo's house, stand in front of the fireplace, and look at the picture of Bottles. Press C-Up and look at Bottles. The picture will give you a word of congratulations and a puzzle game. Play and win the game and Bottles will give you a password. Now do it again and again and again. In all, there are seven puzzles to solve and seven passwords to get. After you've solved all seven puzzles, go back to Treasure Trove Cove and use the Beak Buster on the tiles of the Underwater Castle. Here are the codes, but keep in mind that all codes must be earned before they will work! Note: Puzzle game codes are not saved and must be reentered every time you turn the game off.

Code	What It Does
BOTTLES BONUS ONE	Big head Banjo
BOTTLES BONUS TWO	Big hands Banjo
BOTTLES BONUS THREE	Big head Kazooie
BOTTLES BONUS FOUR	"Hot Dog" Banjo has a stretched-out body

Code	What It Does
BOTTLES BONUS FIVE	Giant Banjo with a small head
BIG BOTTLE BONUS	Giant Banjo and big head Kazooie
NO BONUS	Returns Banjo/ Kazooie to normal
WISHY WASHY BANJO	Banjo turns into a washing machine

Remember: You have to enter the phrases as one word, without spaces in between. And don't try to cheat, either. These codes won't work unless you beat the game. Believe me, I've tried.

GAME NAME: YOSHI'S STORY

ESRB RATING: E for Everyone. Content suitable for those 6 years or older.

THEME: Cartoon adventure

PLAYERS: 1

DEVELOPED BY: Nintendo

COMMENTS: At first glance Yoshi's Story seems to be nothing but a kiddie game. Well, glance again. This is a tough one. It's a 2-D game, rather than 3-D, but the colors and graphics are knockouts. This is the game you can talk your parents into renting for your little brother or sister, then play it yourself. A little kid can play it, but to play it well, you have to be smart. There is lots of stuff in this little kid's game. It's a good adventure.

Yoshi, as you may or may not remember, started off his video life as a Mario sidekick. He's a cute little dino with a long tongue. (Who thinks this stuff up, anyway?) Well, he was so popular as a sidekick that he got his own game, Yoshi's Island, which was a huge, supersmash hit. Now he's back in Yoshi's Story for the N64 system. If nothing else, Yoshi's Story shows that 2-D games are still fun and that everything doesn't have to be 3-D.

The story is simple. Baby Bowser has stolen the Happy Tree from the Yoshi Island and turned the island into a book. A book! Horrors! Anyway, everyone on the island is sad. Except, of course, the six baby Yoshis who were just born. Now they have to rescue the Happy Tree and teach the Baby Bowser a lesson. And they have to do it page by page.

There are six different worlds in Yoshi's Story. Each world has four different levels. Do the math. You'll be going through 24 different adventures or stages.

In each stage you have to find and eat 30 fruit treats. Now, here's the deal. The best fruit to get are the melons. *You have to go after the melons.* There are 30 melons on each stage, and a lot of them can't be found without the R button, which allows Yoshi to smell for clues. Getting the melons allows you to go on to the next level. So, eat as much fruit as you need to keep smiling, but remember, the melons are the key to the game.

Now, here's the other thing. Since it's a one-player game, you'll be playing by yourself. Points don't matter that much in this one-player game. The main thing is to move from one *level* to the next.

The other strategy you might want to consider is going for the same kind of fruit in a row. If you collect any six pieces of the same fruit in a row, then you become Super Happy and are invincible for a while, getting a tongue that's double in length and unlimited eggs to throw. All very handy in any stage of the game.

Another way to get invincible is to get Super Happy eating Heart Fruit that you find. Each is worth eight points.

Different-color Yoshis like different types of fruit. A Yoshi gets more points for eating his favorite fruit. Green Yoshis will get more points when they eat watermelons. Pink/Red Yoshis like apples. Blue/Light blue Yoshis like grapes. Black/White Yoshis like everything. Yellow Yoshis like bananas.

And remember: All Yoshis really, really like melons!

When playing in story mode, you want to collect all three hearts in each level. Collecting these hearts allows you to unlock levels 2, 3, and 4 on the pages in this mode. Do the math. In all, there are 72 hearts. However, without collecting all the hearts, you will not be able to complete all the levels in the next page.

Now, here's the other thing. When you complete a stage, it changes colors on the Map screen. That means you can go back to it in the trial mode. As I mentioned before, points really aren't that important when you move through the game. The main thing is to move from level to level to battle Baby Bowser. However, in trial mode you can go back and try to top your best score.

Tips:

Yes, Yoshi throws eggs in this game. However, be smart about it. Those eggs don't grow on trees. In fact, there are long stretches between eggs during some portions of the game. And remember, you can carry only so many eggs.

Master the Yoshi Hover or Flutter (or whatever you want to call it) by pressing A after jumping. If you do this well, you'll be able to reach heights you never thought possible and recover from falls off platforms.

Turn off the music by turning the volume down on your television. The music, which seems like it's for kiddies, can be annoying after a while and distract you from hunting up the fruit.

GAME NAME: **BOMBERMAN 64**

ESRB RATING: **E for Everyone. Content suitable for those 6 years or older.**

THEME: **Adventure/maze/action**

PLAYERS: **1 or 4**

DEVELOPED BY: **Hudson Soft**

COMMENTS: Mazes. Cute characters. Hidden objects. Nifty puzzles. And bombs! Yeah, lots and lots of bombs. Those of you who played earlier versions of the game may remember hunting around for the really cool bombs. Well, there's no more searching for power-ups to access the cool bombs. Now the bomber dude has a full arsenal. Instead of starting with a single drop-bomb move, you get throwing bombs, kicking bombs, and really big bombs right from the start of the game.

The game features five different worlds and one bonus world, each with four levels, including a volcano, castle, mountains, space station, and medieval village. There really isn't much of a story here. Bomberman's world is invaded, and you have to go through the different worlds to defeat the bad guys. Finally, at the end of the game, you defeat the head bad guy. Big surprise, huh? But who cares? There are bombs in this game, and lots of them. You throw them, drop them, kick them; it all depends on your strategy. Plus, you can play against friends and blow them up. You also can use the bombs to build bridges, create towers, and generally move around the worlds more effectively. However, it takes some practice before you can build with bombs. Give yourself some time to learn all the moves here.

Here's a good tip, though. Remote bombs don't explode until you hit the Z button. You can use these bombs to make ladders and then climb them. Who knew? Well, now you know! The easiest of these techniques is to heave a bomb into a gutter, then use it to step across.

Also, each of the four basic levels of each world can be divided into two categories: killing a boss or searching out goodies. I'm not going to tell you which is which, definitely a spoiler, but be aware of what each level is about and play accordingly. (Big-time Tip: This basic philosophy carries over into a lot of games. A good strategy is to be able to classify a level or world and then plan your play around that classification. Some games mix equal parts of searching and combat, but many do not.)

This game is not about walking around and exploring cool stuff. There are time limits that get tighter as you progress from one world to the next. There are also two difficulty settings. If you play the tougher setting, the bosses are harder to beat and the time limits for finishing a level are less. Don't ignore those time limits.

Finishing a level within the time limit earns you much-needed Gold Cards. However, if you don't finish within the time limit, don't sweat it. You can press Continue. This is a great learning feature, but if you use the continue mode, you won't collect the maximum number of Gold Cards.

Here's the deal for the Gold Cards. Each stage has the potential for five Gold Cards. You can win one by beating all 30 enemies and another for finishing within the time limit. When you defeat a boss or miniboss, he will drop four Gold Cards, five if you beat him in the time limit. *If you collect all 100 cards, then you can move on to the sixth world!*

One of the better features of the game is the ability to start in any of the worlds (except the bonus world) you like. This is pretty cool. It's cool because it allows you to practice and learn the worlds each time you come back to the game. You don't have to learn the game in order; you can learn it in the way that suits you best.

One of the most popular features of previous Bomberman titles was the ability to play against your friends and blow them up. It was pretty cool, and the Bomberman world was pretty small, so getting your friends was easy. Now, with the new version, the idea is to capture all the gems on their side and blow them up. There are some cool options with this. For instance, you can select the number of battles you want

to have and the time limit for each battle.
There's also a Ghost option, which allows a
dead Bomberman to come back, without his
bombs, and jump on the enemy, thus controlling him for a few seconds. This is a pretty cool
option because even though you don't have any
actual bombs as a ghost, you can cause your
opponent to run into an exploding bomb thrown
by someone else.

The strategy also has changed. The playing
field is *soooo* much bigger, so you can't blow
up opponents as easily. First you have to stun
them by hitting them with a bomb and then
have the bomb explode close to them. Tough,
but it can be done.

Tips:

The A button doubles a bomb's power. If you
tap the B button when Bomberman has a bomb
in his hands, the bomb will start to grow. Stop
when it turns yellow.

Don't think you can play the game in normal
mode, memorize the locations of all the Gold
Cards, then go into hard mode and remember
where all the cards are located. When you move
into hard mode, the locations of the cards
change.

When your Bomberman is stunned by a
bomb or hit with something, rotate the control
stick rapidly for a faster recovery. This is also
a good way to get rid of those pesky ghosts that

attack you when playing against friends.

By pressing the B button, Bomberman can catch objects being thrown at him.

Bomberman isn't just limited to bombs. He can pick up opponents and throw them off high places. This is true when playing against friends or the CPU.

There are bunches of Bomberman features to pick up in virtually every level, such as high-tops and a drill arm. Go for it, you'll be glad you did.

Secret Codes:

How fast is your controller finger? Well, it better be plenty fast to enter this code. Go to the menu and to the option that reads Adventure/ Battle Custom options. Select Battle and then press the Start button really fast. If you do it right you'll hear a chime and get four more battlefields to choose from.

Bomberman Codes:

Credits Preview: This really isn't a code, but it's still pretty good. After you collect all the Gold Cards (easy, right?) and beat Sirius in the Rainbow Palace (no problem!), go to the Options screen and select Options. You can now preview the ending and credits whenever you like. So what if it isn't the greatest thing since sliced bologna, it's still cool.

When you get all 120 Gold Cards, a new

option will appear in the Options menu that will let you to enter each level with Super Out Remote Controlled. To get Ultra Bombs, rotate your customized Bomberman in the main screen, press Z to go clockwise and R to go counterclockwise.

THE BEST OF THE REST: ADVENTURE RPG

GAME NAME: **Chameleon Twist: Eating the Final Boss**

ESRB RATING: **E for Everyone. Content suitable for those 6 years or older.**

THEME: **Fantasy/adventure**

PLAYERS: **1 to 4**

DEVELOPED BY: **Japan System Supply**

PUBLISHED BY: **Sunsoft**

COMMENTS: Here's one of those games that all the Look-at-me, I'm-so-serious players like to turn up their noses at. Me? I happen to like it. It's kind of a fun game. You choose between four different lizards—uh, chameleons—uh, kids with lizard tongues—and let go with your tongue at weird enemies, like an ice cream sandwich. The game has been compared to Mario, Bomberman, and Yoshi. It's a kind of fight-and-explore game. There are six different worlds (plus a bonus world) to explore, and you don't have to do them in any particular order.

However, you also can load the game as a four-player and beat each other up with lizard tongues. You can play the multiplayer in either a timed mode or a sudden-death battle-to-the-end mode.

If you're having trouble with some of the tougher games, like Mario 64, and are sick of never being able to finish them, then this is a pretty good place to practice. Plus, with a little effort you'll get to the end.

Bonus Level: Yes, there is a Bonus level. To access it, you have to get at least 20 crowns from each level. After you do that, a Question Mark box will appear over the first stage. There are six pictures, one of each boss. Jump through the picture to fight the bosses.

Play Pool Bonus: If you have at least 50 crowns by the time you get to Level 6, go to the Ghost Castle, but don't go directly up the stairs. Instead, go to the rabbit; there's a door near the crown. The door will open only if you have 50 crowns, but inside you get to play a game of pool with the boss.

GAME NAME: GLOVER
ESRB RATING: E for Everyone. Content suitable for those 6 years or older.
THEME: Adventure/puzzle
PLAYERS: 1

DEVELOPED BY: Interactive Studios

PUBLISHED BY: Hasbro Interactive

COMMENTS: Glover is kind of a goofy game. You either like it or you don't. It's an adventure puzzle game where you are Glover the Glove. Okay, so you're an enchanted glove. Truthfully, you're the Good Guy Glove. (There's also a Bad Guy Glove out there.) The object of the game is to explore the seven worlds provided and gather up a variety of balls. You can bounce them, roll them, or transform them with magic powers to make them easier to move around. That's pretty much it. If you read this far and the idea of gloves doesn't sound all that great, then forget it. This is a great game for the player who is just starting out on adventure, puzzle, and maze kinds of games. So, if some of the more complicated videos have got you down, then you might want to give Glover a try. Okay, I'll admit it—Glover does look pretty cool bouncing the balls or crawlin' around.

Codes:

Ball Control: For controlling the ball: Press Start while playing and then enter: C-Left, C-Right, C-Left, C-Right, C-Up, C-Down, C-Right, C-Right.

Fish-Eye: To create a fish-eye view from the camera, during game play enter: C-Left, C-

Right, C-Left, C-Right, C-Left, C-Right, C-Left, C-Right.

Low Gravity: To create an extra-bouncy, low-gravity environment, press Start to pause the game and enter: C-Left, C-Left, C-Up, C-Left, C-Right, C-Up, C-Up, C-Up.

Play as a Froggy: To play as the frog: Press Start to pause game play then enter C-Up, C-Right, C-Down, C-Right, C-Up, C-Left, C-Left, C-Up. (Note: While playing as the frog you can gain extra lives by eating insects.)

Powerball: To create a Powerball, pause the game by pressing Start and enter: C-Up, C-Down, C-Up, C-Down, C-Up, C-Down, C-Left, C-Up.

Rotate Camera View: Pause the game and enter: C-Left, C-Right, C-Up, C-Up, C-Down, C-Right, C-Down, C-Right

Unlimited Energy: For unlimited energy: press Start to pause the game, then enter: C-Right, C-Right, C-Down, C-Right, C-Right, C-Right, C-Up, C-Left.

PUZZLES AND OTHER GAMES

GAME NAME: BUST-A-MOVE 2

ESRB RATING: E for Everyone. Content suitable for those 6 years or older.

THEME: Puzzle game

PLAYERS: 1 or 2

DEVELOPED BY: Probe

PUBLISHED BY: Acclaim

COMMENTS: A classic puzzle game where the objective is to clear the screen of marbles by busting them up. This is a very cool game and a lot like Tetris.

Codes:

Selecting Special Characters When in Mode: When you begin a game in puzzle mode, move your cursor to A or B (indicating the first puzzle you want to try). Then press Left, Left, Up, Down, Left, Right, Left, Right. Then press the L and R buttons at the same time and hold them. You should see a Character Select screen. Use your control pad to select the character you want to play as, then highlight and press A.

More Puzzles: Go to the Title screen and press the left button on the control pad. Then press the right and down on pad. You should see the little green guy in the bottom of the screen. Next go to puzzle mode; there should be an option for Another World. That world contains a bunch more puzzles.

GAME NAME: IGGY'S RECKIN' BALLS

ESRB RATING: E for Everyone. Content suitable for those 6 years or older.

THEME: Racing balls

PLAYERS: 1 to 4

DEVELOPED BY: Iguana

PUBLISHED BY: Acclaim

COMMENTS: A race game where you don't race cars, planes, motorcycles, or Jet Skis. You race balls. Okay, it sounds goofy, but it's a lot of fun. One to four players can race at once and choose from 17 different ball racers. Sometimes you just want to play a weird game, right? Well, here it is!

Codes:

To get to the cheat screen, go to the main menu and press Z and R together. After you type in a code, press Start to activate it. If you've entered correctly, you'll hear a confirmation tone. If you've entered it incorrectly, you won't hear anything. If you want to turn a code on or off during the game, pause it and you'll be taken to the Cheat screen. Note: You can use all codes any time you want, except "ICEPRINCESS."

All Secret Characters (well, almost all secret characters): HAPPYHEADS

All Worlds Available: UNIVERSE

Dark Mode: 2ROKTOO

Fat Character Mode: TOOMUCHPIE

Pencil Mode: ROLFHARRIS

Random Fashion Statements and Changes: SWOSHOP

Slippery Mode: ICEPRINCESS

Super Turbo Meter: GOBABY

Tiny Mode: MICROBALLS

GAME NAME: TETRISPHERE

ESRB RATING: E for Everyone. Content suitable for those 6 years or older.

THEME: Puzzle

PLAYERS: 1 or 2

DEVELOPED BY: H2O

PUBLISHED BY: Nintendo

COMMENTS: This is an updated, 3-D version of the video arcade classic. You have to fit the dropping pieces of the puzzle together for points. I know it sounds a little boring, but it isn't.

Tip:

Your parents may let you rent or buy this one more easily because they remember the original Tetris and secretly want to play this version. If that happens, then learn all the secret codes and really amaze them.

Codes:

A Weird Scene: Go to the main menu, choose Single, then select New Game option and enter the name "VORTEX." Confirm the name and then press and keep pressed the reset button. After a little while you'll see characters from the game getting sucked into—what else?—a vortex.

Access Bonus Music: Go to the main menu and select Single. Then go to New Name and change the characters on the screen by punching in: C-Right, C-Down, and L all at once. Once you have accessed the new character, enter your name as "G(Alien Head)MEBOY." The Alien Head will replace the A in GAME-BOY.

Bonus Game: To play a bonus game that is similar to Rescue, go to the New Game screen and enter Single. Then, under New Name, put in "LINES." A new game will appear under the Versus CPU option along with instructions about how to play it.

Level Select: To enter any level you want in rescue, hide and seek, and puzzle modes, go to the main menu and select Single. Select New Name. Then press L, C-Down, and C-Right all at once. A new set of characters will appear. Enter your name as Saturn(planet), UFO, Rocket, Heart, and Skull.

View Ending Credits: Go to the main menu and select Single. Then choose New Name and enter "CREDITS" as your name.

THE BEST OF THE REST: PUZZLE AND OTHER GAMES

GAME NAME: VIRTUAL CHESS 64

ESRB RATING: E for Everyone. Content suitable for those 6 years or older.

THEME: **Chess. Yes, chess!**

PLAYERS: **1 to 4**

PUBLISHED BY: **Titus**

COMMENTS: Chess, right? *Boring!* Wrong! This is chess as cool as it gets. When pieces go to war, they really fight it out. This is chess for one to four players. So you can play against the CPU or up to four players can play at once. This is an excellent video game to learn the chess basics or to sharpen your game.

Codes:

Not a lot of secret codes for this game. After all, it is chess. However, to hear the CPU unit *think* over its moves during a game, press C-Up, C-Down, C-Left, C-Right, Joypad-Up, Joypad-Down, Joypad-Left, Joypad-Right.

GAME NAME: **MILO'S ASTRO LANES**

ESRB RATING: **E for Everyone. Content suitable for those 6 years or older.**

THEME: **Bowling**

PLAYERS: **1 to 4**

PUBLISHED BY: **Crave Entertainment**

COMMENTS: This is bowling the way it's sup-posed to be—weird. Very strange lanes and even stranger rules. There's some kind of story that goes along with this game, but it's boring, so I won't mention it because it might sound boring to you, too. The point is, you should give this little game a chance. It's got some really fine points, including old-fashioned cartoon kind of graphics. You get to choose from six characters (Milo is the most boring) and work your way up 12 lanes that get stranger and stranger. There are also 12 Astro Balls that do some pretty cool tricks. And there are three different play modes: elimination, puzzle, and multiplayer. So, lace up your funny shoes and get bowling.

First off, there are three different types of lanes: Novice, Expert, and Cosmic class with lanes that aren't even flat, but have hills and bumps in them. Also, the old rules don't apply. Not only are the lanes weirdly shaped, like corkscrews and U-turns, but players throw stuff, like acid and bombs, at an opponent's ball.

Codes:

After you enter these codes, you will hear a confirmation tone to tell you that you did it correctly.

Booster Ball (gives more speed): R, R, L, L, R, L.

Clone Ball (splits into three balls): L, L, L, R, R, R.

Mega Ball (grows to giant size): L, L, R, R, L, R.

White Dwarf Ball (gives more weight and knocking-down power): R, R, R, L, L, L.

ACTION

FIGHTING

GAME NAME: WWF WARZONE

ESRB RATING: T for Teen. Content suitable for those 13 years or older.

THEME: Professional wrestling

PLAYERS: 1 to 4

DEVELOPED BY: Acclaim

COMMENTS: If you still think professional wrestling is real, then either grow up or start planning for the Easter Bunny!

This is probably the only video game that is more real than the so-called sport it is modeled on. Developed by Acclaim, WWF has 18 World Wrestling Federation wrestlers (including two hidden) and eight modes. One to four players can take to the ring and fight it out for the championship.

This is a game that definitely has depth. There are so many features, cheats, and codes that if you were stranded on a desert island, this is the game you'd want to have along.

Now, remember, it would be best if you were stranded on an island with a Nintendo 64 system, color television, and electricity.

It's impossible to list all of the strategies, codes, and cheats in the space allowed, so I'm just going to list some of my favorites, even some of the dumb ones.

Modes:

Training Mode: It sounds like wimp city, but the smart player spends time here perfecting his grappling skills. The more time you spend in training mode learning the moves, the more you'll kick butt in the game. Trust me on this fact. WarZone is a tough game to master, and the training mode can be your best friend. With so many moves, including takedowns, finishers, and combos, the winner will be the one who spends time in this mode. The good folks at Acclaim have rigged the mode so that you can practice a specific move or situation. You can even set the training opponent to stand up or lie down to practice your moves.

Challenge: This one-player mode allows you to win your way to the championship. However, once you reach the Contender level, you have only three chances at the championship. Warning: As you make your way up the WWF rankings, foes from past bouts will challenge you to rematches. When does the challenge mode end?

Never! You have to quit the game to make it stop. After you win the championship, you keep fighting to defend it.

Cage Match: For up to four players. Any fan of wrestling knows what a Cage Match is all about. This cage happens to be held high in the air. You can climb outside the cage, but why give your opponent a chance to knock you off? Best strategy is to make use of the cage by climbing around the inside and diving on your opponent.

Royal Rumble: One to four players can play toss the opponent in this mode. The rules are simple: The last player left in the ring wins.

Versus: One or two players take on wrestlers the computer picks.

Tag Team: Action for one to four players. Strategy is the name of the game in this mode. It's essential that you time your tagging of partner before your energy is depleted.

Weapons: One to four players can go at it with bats, chairs, and television monitors. It's ugly and it's brutal, so don't get caught napping at the controls.

Gauntlet: One-player mode in which you take on six challengers, one right after another.

Sounds easy, right? Wrong! If you get hurt in one match, the injury counts in the following match, and the following match, and the match after that, too. Strategy and smart wrestling is the name of the game in this mode.

War: This mode takes three or four players for an all-out battle. The last man standing in the ring wins.

Strategy/Tips:

Warning: Opponents may be closer than they appear! Get your ranges right. Opponents who look like they are too far away to attack effectively can surprise you.

Down, But Not Out!: Opponents are tricky. When you knock an adversary down, be sure to back away quickly, unless he is stunned. (Check the Stun Meter.) The computer's wrestlers are programmed to attack from the mat. If he is stunned, then try another attack. Again, check the Stun Meter to see if you have time for another attack or a pin.

Pinning Takes Patience: As every wrestling fan knows, there are no quick pins in professional wrestling. Never, ever try to pin an opponent unless his Health Meter is in the red; otherwise he will surprise you.

Take Your Chances: To have the system choose a wrestler for you at the Selection screen, all you have to do is hold Up and then Kick.

Stupid Wrestling Tricks:

Let's assume you're bored with all the butt-wumping violence of the game. Maybe you could use a good laugh . . . okay, a cheap chuckle would even be good. Here's a list of some of the weirder options built into War-Zone. Odd? Yes. Tasteless? Certainly. Funny? You bet! Educational? Not a chance! But, hey, this is professional wrestling we're talking about here!

Big Head Mode: Beat the challenge mode on medium difficulty with either the Rock or British Bulldog and you can activate this weird mode in which all the wrestlers will have really *big heads*. Why? Who cares? It's funny. Similar to this is the ego mode, which is activated when you beat the challenge on medium difficulty with Ahmed Johnson. The more you damage your opponent, the bigger your head gets.

Pull My Finger Mode: Beat the challenge on medium difficulty with a Headbanger (either Thrasher or Mosh) and the wrestlers will come down with a really, really bad case of gas when they are hit. Gamers have taken to calling this the beans mode.

Maddening Crowd: Start a match with no computerized players. Just leave the wrestlers standing without doing anything. The crowd will get extremely angry, and J.R. and Vince will add some timely lines. If you think this sounds like a waste of time, then you're right. But it's still funny.

Glossy Mat Mode: Beat the challenge level on medium difficulty with any character. Makes the wrestling mat have a shiny gloss to it. Not a great trick, but worth a try if you're bored.

How do you get a virtual crowd cheering for you in WWF? Why, by taunting your opponent, of course. These combinations work for all wrestlers during the match with a few easy-to-master moves:

Taunt 1: Press: Punch, Block.

Taunt 2: Press: Tie-Up, Kick.

Needless to Say, Shawn Michaels Has Extra Taunts: Position Michaels leaning back on the ropes, choose HBK for a character in any game mode. Then approach the ropes and press: A, C-Left. Michaels should jump on the ropes and yell: "I'm gonna dance all over your face!" Then get Michaels on top of the turnbuckle and press: Punch, Block. He'll flex his muscles.

Clone Alone: Let your creative talents run wild and crazy in the create a wrestler mode. While most people look to create the baddest guy in the ring, others look to make up the weirdest. Both are noble ambitions, but the creation mode also lets you create clones from other games that look almost exactly like the real thing. Following are codes for Lara Croft and Duke Nukem, but feel free to experiment on your own.

Lara Croft	Duke Nukem
Gender: Female	Gender: Male
Face: 2	Body type: Muscle
Hair: Pullback	Face: 1
Shirt: (tanktop) Adventure	Hair: Auburn
Pants: (shorts) Safari	Tanktop: Generic 1
Belt: Chain 2	Pants: Denim
Boots Chain 2	Belt: Stud
Gloves: Finger	Boots: Black
Accessories: Sunglasses 3	Armpads: Gray
	Accessories: Sunglasses 3

No Meters Mode: Beat the challenge mode on medium difficulty with the Undertaker. There are no energy bars, stun meters, or the like when this cheat is activated.

Ladies Night: Beat the challenge mode on medium difficulty with Shawn Michaels or Triple H. Provides a female template in create a wrestler mode.

Clothes But No Cigar: What's wrestling without weird costumes? That's right, without the costumes it's just a bunch of guys with big muscles beating the boogers out of each other. So, in the grand tradition of professional wrestling, the programmers at Acclaim included a whole bunch of costume tricks for WarZone. The majority of the wrestlers have two outfit choices. To select your first outfit, hold C-Down when choosing your wrestler or just choose him normally. For the wrestler's second outfit, hold C-Right while you choose him. To access additional outfits for Austin or Goldust, hold Top R when choosing their third costume. For their fourth outfit, hold C-Up when choosing.

Different-Color Costumes: Hold C-Left, C-Right, C-Up, C-Down, and press A at the Character Selection screen under the medium or hard level.

Oh Shirt!: Win the WWF title in challenge mode as Kane in medium or hard level and additional shirts, jackets, masks, pants, and more clothes will be available in create a wrestler mode. Winning one-player challenge mode unlocks a lot of extra costumes in the create mode,

including demonic clown masks, skeleton outfits, alien heads, and more!

Alternate Goldust Costumes: Win the title in
challenge mode with Goldust in medium or
hard levels and hold L2, R1, or R2 while selecting Goldust on the character selection
screen. You'll get more costume choices, including the Marilyn Dust and Dusty Dust versions.

Easy Ring Out: As the match starts, climb down
from the ring with your opponent following.
Then get your opponent to follow you around
the outside of the ring as the time ticks away.
However, don't get too far ahead of the opponent, 'cause he'll just get bored and climb back
into the ring. When the timer gets to five seconds, hit your opponent until he becomes
stunned. While he's still stunned, jump back on
the mat with only a second or two left on the
clock and your character should win by ring
out. This low-down, cheap way of winning
takes some practice, but it does work.

Continue Wrestling After Match Ends: Call in another wrestler for help during a match and then
let that wrestler defeat your opponent. Be sure
to jump out of the ring just when your opponent
is about to be pinned. You'll be able to hit your
opponent from the floor as long as you want.
Walk on the edge of the ring to end the match.

Female Wrestler: To create a female wrestler, complete challenge mode with Shawn Michaels. It takes practice to beat Michaels, so this isn't such an easy trick to pull off. Then head back down to the create mode and pick a wrestler. Also, winning one-player challenge mode with Triple H or HBK unlocks female wrestlers in the create modes as well as all sorts of female clothes. Rumor has it that you can put these clothes on the male wrestlers as well, though nobody I know has confessed to this.

Get More Attribute Points: An easy way to get more attribute points when creating a wrestler is to load the wrestler and exit the create mode. Then, after you win a match with your created wrestler, you have two extra attribute points. Go back to the create mode and claim your points.

An Even Easier Way to Get More Attribute Points: Choose and edit your created wrestler and save. Then load the wrestler again, but leave the Create screen on. Immediately reenter the create mode and choose to create a character. The wrestler you created should have the same amount of attribute points as the saved character. Then save the new character under a different file.

For those of you who don't want to earn 40 points with each and every one of your created wrestlers, just complete the task with one of them and then create the others by loading your first wrestler, changing him, and then saving him in a new slot.

My Favorite Special and Finishing Moves:

All moves must be done when the opponent's life bar indicator is red. Also, when a move is listed with a yellow and green direction, you can use either one.

Ahmed Johnson's Pearl River Plunge: Right, Left, Up, Kick, Block (while both wrestlers are standing).

Bret Hart's Sharpshooter: Left, Left, Up, Kick, Block (while opponent is grounded).

Davey Boy "British Bulldog" Smith Running Powerslam: Up, Down, Tie-Up (while wrestling).

Faarooq's Dominator: Up, Up, Up, Tie-Up, Block (while wrestling).

Golddust's Curtain Call: Right, Down, Down, Tie-Up, Block (while wrestling).

Headbanger Mosh: Left, Right, Up, Tie-Up, Block (from top of turnbuckle).

Headbanger Thrasher Stage Dive: Right, Up, Up, Punch, Kick (standing on top of turnbuckle).

Kane's Tombstone: Down, Down, Down, Punch, and Tie-Up (while standing beside) or Up, Down, Tie-Up (while wrestling).

Ken Shamrock's Ankle Submission: Left, Right, Up, Kick, Tie-Up.

Mankind's Mandible Claw 1: Left, Right, Up, Tie-Up, and Block (while close to opponent).

Mankind's Mandible Claw 2: Left, Right, Tie-Up (while wrestling).

Mankind's Mandible Claw 3: Left, Right, Up, Tie-Up, and Block (while opponent is down on the mat).

Ol' Mick Foley Version: Winning one player challenge mode with Mankind unlocks the Cactus Jack and Dude Love versions of ol' Mick Foley.

Owen "The Black Hart" Hart's Sharpshooter: Left, Left, Up, Kick, Block.

Owen Hart Extra Hurrican-ranna: When running, press B and C-Down as you come very close to your opponent. Owen will jump on opponent's shoulders and give out a Hurrican-ranna.

Shawn "Heartbreak Kid" Michaels Sweet Chin Music: Right, Down, Up, Kick, Block (while both wrestlers are standing).

Steve Austin's Stone Cold Stunner: Right, Right, Up, Tie-Up, and Block (while wrestling).

The Rock's Rock Bottom: Right, Right, Up, Punch, and Tie-Up (while standing).

Triple H's Pedigree: Left, Down, Right, Punch, and Tie-Up (while wrestling).

Bret Hart's Sharpshooter: Left, Left, Up, Kick, Block, and X (while opponent is grounded).

GAME NAME: FIGHTER'S DESTINY

ESRB RATING: T for Teen. Content suitable for those 13 years or older.

THEME: Fighting

PLAYERS: 1 or 2

DEVELOPED BY: Imagineer/Genki/Ocean

COMMENTS: I'm a simple kind of guy. Any fighting game where you get to go one-on-one with a cow is okay with me. Face it, how many times have you sat down with your friends and said, "You know, I sure wish there was a good fighting game with a cow in it''? Maybe your friends started edging nervously away from you. But if you're like me, a dreamer, a romantic, and a lover of fighting games and cows, then you know what I'm talking about. Fighting video games and cows. They just go together. Think about it—but not for too long.

How about beating the boogers out of a clown? Yeah, now we're talking. But seriously, all kidding aside, this is an excellent fighting game. And if you like fighting games, this is probably one that you missed in all the hype surrounding the high-profile, superviolent games. It doesn't get into that weird, slasher-movie kind of bloodshed. You need a certain amount of skill to play this game, but not so much that you'll spend the rest of your life trying to learn the ten-button combo moves. Plus, there are enough modes and player options to keep you going.

There are ten fighters and a slew of hidden fighters, each with his own style and moves. And while a lot of the fighters share certain moves, the fighting styles include, well, everything. You have high-flying artists, karate, professional wrestling, boxing—everything!

There are five basic modes. In the versus mode, you play against the computer as it lines up one opponent after another for you. In the battle mode, you fight an opponent to gain his or her skills. The record attack mode includes three different kinds of battles. The first allows you to select from survival mode and fight 100 fights in a row to win. A timed mode lets you try to beat your best times for victory. And then there is something called Rodeo in which you fight a cow kind of character called Ushi. Then there's the master challenge mode, where you face 12 CPU-controlled opponents divided up into Masters. If you beat the Masters, you get their skills. If you beat the Jokers, you get nothing. But if you lose to the Jokers, you lose some of your skills. (Mean Cheater's Trick: Get all the skills from the master challenge mode. Save them, then challenge a friend to a little one-on-one. You'll have a real advantage with all those saved skills.) Last, there's a training mode with a robot called Robert—call him Robby for short. This is actually a good skill-building mode. Don't sell it short. They say that there are more than 60 moves per character. I never mastered even close to that many, but I believe them. The Robot can save you a lot of frustration if you practice with him.

Now, here's the really cool thing about the game. It's based on a point system. To win a match, you have to score seven (count 'em, seven!) points. You win points by knocking your opponent down, depleting his life bar, and using special moves. And, for those who are interested, you can win by throwing an opponent out of the ring.

Okay, so you don't like the rules? Fine. Change them. This game has an amazing col-

lection of things you can customize, including
the size of the ring and points awarded.

Strategy:

Be prepared to plan your attacks. You just can't
knock someone down that easily. First soften
him up with a bunch of hits, getting him dizzy,
then go in for the knockdown. And keep your
eye on those meters.

What's the most annoying thing someone can
do to you in a fighting game? No, not that!
What I mean is, someone who just kinda
hunches down and doesn't do anything. He just
sits there like a lump, crouching and blocking.
It's annoying, right? Of course it is. But Destiny has this cool little gauge that pops up when
someone is about to throw you. If you get one
of these guys on Destiny, then go to throw him.
It's virtually impossible to keep from getting
thrown if he has his finger jammed down on
the block button. He either fights or gets
thrown.

Forget about going head-to-head with the
cow. The cow is bigger and stronger and will
kick your butt. You have to fight the cow smart.
Vallerie and her high-flying routine will do the
job. The cow isn't that fast and certainly can't
match the airborne skills. Cows don't fly.

Codes and Tricks:

The game lets you choose a bunch of secret
fighters and former opponents. The trick (yes,

there's always a trick) is that you have to have a star next to your name showing that you beat the game.

Avoid the Joker in Master Challenge: This seems to work, but it could be luck. To avoid picking the Joker, choose before the wheel picks up speed.

Change Outfits: To change your fighter's clothes, go to the Select screen and hold down the R button.

Play as Boro: Beat the game on the easy mode.

Play as Robert the Training Robot: Go into the fastest mode and beat all the fighters in less than one minute. That's not one minute for each fighter, that's one minute for all of them.

Play as the Joker: This is a tough one. You have to beat all 100 opponents in survival mode to get the Joker as a playable character.

Play as the Master: Beat everyone in the master challenge mode with any character and you'll be able to play as the Master.

Play as Ushi the Cow: Get to the rodeo mode by beating the game and earning a star. Then stay alive for at least a minute in Record Attack (not as easy as it sounds) and you will be able to play as the cow. Careful, though; don't kill the cow or it won't work.

THE BEST OF THE REST: FIGHTING GAMES

GAME NAME: **CLAY FIGHTER 63⅓**

ESRB RATING: **T for Teen. Content suitable for those 13 years or older.**

THEME: **Silly fighting game**

PLAYERS: **1 or 2**

DEVELOPED BY: **Interplay Productions**

COMMENTS: Hey, where's my Nintendo 63⅓ system? Sheesh, I can't play this game without that. This is a very, very silly fighting game. A lot of people don't like it, but really, it's a load of laughs.

Codes:

Let Computer Choose Your Fighter: Press L and R simultaneously on the Character Select screen and the CPU will choose your fighter.

Ring Selection Feature: When you want to play a two-player Versus match, go to the Versus screen. Either player can then press a C button and the Stage Select feature will come up. After you choose a ring you'd like to fight in, then press the B button.

Secret Options Code: To get to the secret options mode, go to the Character Select screen, then hold the L button while pressing C-Up, C-Right, C-Left, C-Down, B, A, A. The screen will flash. After you see the flash, press the B button to return to the Title screen, which should now include Secret Options under Select Options. This code opens a whole new dimension in Clay Fighters for you. Among the Secret Options you can choose from are:

A. Background choice for one-play mode.
B. Body-type choices, including normal, huge, and small.
C. Voice changes, including normal, high, or low.
D. Camera flights: Turns on/off the stage flying camera at the beginning of each match.
E. Claytality: A fatality timer for the game can be turned on or off, giving players either a limited or unlimited time to complete a Claytality.
F. Ability to move the camera using a fourth controller.

Play as Sumo Santa: Go to the Character Select screen, hold down the L button and enter: A, C-Down, C-Right, C-Up, C-Left, B. The screen will flash and the Sumo Santa will be a playable character.

Play as Dr. Kiln Code: Go to the Character Select screen, hold down the L button and enter: B,

C-Left, C-Up, C-Right, C-Down, A. The screen will flash and the Dr. Kiln Code will be a playable character.

GAME NAME: **CLAY FIGHTER: SCULPTOR'S CUT**

ESRB RATING: **T for Teen. Content suitable for those 13 years or older.**

THEME: **Clay fighting figures**

PLAYERS: **1 or 2**

PUBLISHED BY: **Interplay**

COMMENTS: This game has it all: thrills, chills, mindless violence and clay figures beating each other up. *This is the only game that dares to have a character named Boogerman!* Does Tekken have Boogerman? Does Mortal Kombat have Boogerman? Do any of those other fancy-pants games with all their combos and jumping around have him? The answer is no, absolutely not! And I tell you this, sincerely, truthfully, and from the bottom of my heart—Boogerman is awesome. I say pick Boogerman today! A follow-up to Clay Fighter 63⅓, the game that only a few discriminating experts liked, Sculptor's Cut is available for rental only at Blockbuster. This game features more digital horsepower than 63⅓. Sculptor's also has better graphics and more characters. And it has Boogerman!

Codes:

(including the Secret Code to Unlocking the One and Only Boogerman Character):

Play as Boogerman: At the Character Select screen, hold Z (or L shift) and then press B, B, C-Right, C-Right, C-Left, C-Right). To access Boogerman, press R Shift while the cursor is on the question mark.

Play as Earthworm Jim: Go to the Character Select screen, hold Z (or L Shift), and then press B, C-Left, C-Up, C-Right, C-Down, C-Up. You'll hear a confirmation tone. Then press R Shift when the cursor is on the question mark.

Play as High Five: Go to the Character Select screen, hold Z (or L Shift), and then press B, C-Left, C-Up, C-Right, C-Down, C-Up. You'll hear a confirmation tone. Then press R Shift while the cursor is on the question mark.

Play as Sumo Santa: Go to the Character Select screen at the beginning of the game. Then hold down Z (or L Shift) and press A, C-Right, A, C-Right, C-Down, C-Up. You'll hear a confirmation tone. Then press R Shift while the cursor is on the question mark.

COMBAT GAMES

GAME NAME: BLAST CORPS

ESRB RATING: E for Everyone. Content suitable for those 6 years or older.

THEME: Combat/action

PLAYERS: 1

DEVELOPED BY: Nintendo/Rare

COMMENTS: Here's a game that isn't about blowing anything up. The idea is to *keep* stuff from blowing up. Hey, but don't confuse the action in this game with sitting around knitting with your aunt Edna. There's a lot of action here. Tons of it. This game is about knocking down buildings. Yeah! This one-player action game also has a great plot. A truck filled with nuclear explosives is out of control in the streets. Your job is to knock down buildings before it can bump into anything and explode. Including seven bonus missions, there are over 50 levels in this bad puppy. There are eight wrecking vehicles, four cars, a bunch of other stuff, like a train, a flying robot thing called J-Bomb, and a missile-launching motorcycle to drive. There are also a bunch of training levels, so you can make yourself an expert in each of the vehicles. This is absolutely one of the best games for Nintendo around.

Tips:

(Note: You should attempt to find the scientists only after completing your primary mission.)

Argent Towers Scientist: Find the gray block and push it out of the way and go down the ramp/walkway. Move the TNT crate against the wooden door. Blow up the door and go through it. There's a train on the other side. Get into the train and drive forward. Then get into the Ballista bike and ride it up the central street. Go back to the block, get off, and walk back down to the tunnel. Across from the tower on the right turn left, and you'll go into a maze and get into the police car. The scientist is in a trailer in the lower left-hand part of the maze.

Walk-Throughs:

I know, I know, I said I hated walk-throughs. But this is a really tough game, and these walk-throughs are fun.

Bonus Levels: Complete every mission and rescue the survivors and you get a bonus of two extra courses.

Easy Explosion: Drive up next to a building and try to get your driver out of the vehicle. You do this by pressing Z. You have to maneuver just right and not get too close. However, if you are properly positioned, your driver will yell (keep holding Z down) and the building will come down. This may not work on all buildings, but for those it does work on, it's a great time saver.

Ebony Coast Scientist: Use the Ramdozer to push the TNT to the wall blocking the train. Then push the TNT on to the train. Then get on the train and reverse it, riding it back until you are near the statue. J-Bomb should now be fairly easy to find. Take J-Bomb to the first tunnel and fly up and out over the hill. The scientist is in his trailer to the right.

Fast Start: During those parts of the game where your performance is timed, you can get a better start off the line by pressing the accelerator on the last beep as the light turns green. This may take some practice, but the time you will save is worth it.

Ghost Image: After finishing a racing-type level, go back and do the race again. Notice anything weird? That car you're racing against is the same car you drove the last time.

Glory Crossing: Toward the end of the level, find the tunnel at the west side. The scientist is to the left. Hey, that was easier than you thought it would be, huh? Use the orange truck to get to the tunnel.

Inventory: There are so many things to blow up, knock down, and find, it's tough to keep track of them all. After you feel you've completed a course, then go back to the World Map screen. The course will be circled. If it's circled in red, then you got everything and should move on. However, if it's circled in green, that means you've missed something. Go back and start looking.

Ironstone Mike (a very tough level): Get off the train and go right until you get to the Ramdozer that is hidden in a kind of cut in the mountain. Ride it to the path along the mountainside and find the crane. Load the Ramdozer to the other side of the tracks. Go across the bridge and get into the Ramdozer. Now push the TNT into the building and blow it up. It'll reveal a tunnel. Go straight back in the maze, then turn down the last path before the wall. It will lead to the scientist.

Oyster Harbor: Get into the first barge, go to the small island, and find the scientist. Actually, it's not that easy. First you have to have gotten the TNT on to the barge earlier in the level. Now take it off the barge and use it to blow up the blocks near the third barge, freeing your craft so it can go into the open sea.

Tempest City (requires a lot of ammo): After stocking up on ammo, go to the right-hand side down in the corner. Move along the fence and destroy the main light, then destroy the central (middle) wall. Just keep firing at it. Go up the ramp behind the knocked-down wall and destroy the boxes. The scientist's trailer is behind the boxes.

THE BEST OF THE REST: COMBAT GAMES

GAME NAME: **STAR WARS: SHADOWS OF THE EMPIRE**

ESRB RATING: **Rating T for Teen. Content suitable for those 13 years or older.**

THEME: **Intergalactic combat (what else?)**

PLAYERS: **1**

DEVELOPED BY: **LucasArts**

PUBLISHED BY: **Nintendo**

COMMENTS: Yeah, yeah, yeah—long time ago, in a galaxy far, far away—got it, been there, and done that. But what you really want to know is if this one-player game is any good, right? Well, it rocks! It has ten stages and four levels. Fans of the movie will not be disappointed. This is pure Star Wars with a few twists and surprises. There's a story in the game, but I don't want to ruin it for you. Let's just say, everyone you want to be in the game will be in the game. One word of warning, though: This isn't an easy game to master. Start off slow and work your way up in skill levels . . . and may the Force be with you.

Cheats:

This is *the major* cheat of the game. You really should to do this—or at least try to do it. But it's a tough one, so get a friend to read the directions while you push the buttons. I'll walk you through it, but it may take some practice before you get it right. If you manage to get this code input correctly—and it's tough to do— then you get a bunch of neat powers, like invincibility, the ability to walk through walls, a teleport, and other stuff. If you can't get it input or if the darned thing doesn't work, don't sweat it too much. You can win the game without the extras.

Enter the player's name as "(one space) Wampa(two spaces)Stompa." That's one blank before Wampa and two blanks after Wampa. Make sure you capitalize the W and the S. Got all that? Good, 'cause it gets tougher. Start playing the game (it doesn't matter where) and pause. Then hold down all of the following buttons at the same time: C, Z, L, R, and joypad Left. Keep going, you're almost there.

Now, in a loud, clear Darth Vadar voice, say:

"Luke, I am your father." This won't actually do anything, but you should never miss an opportunity to do a Darth impersonation. Okay, back to the code. Push the joystick to the left until you hear a confirmation. When you hear the tone, let go of the stick. Repeat the process, but move the stick to the right. You'll hear another confirmation tone. Now repeat again to the left and then again to the right, and once again to (you guessed it), the left. Just a little more, you can do it.

Finally, you should see some reddish/pink-ish/orangish printing at the top of the screen. Now follow instructions and use the L and R buttons to switch options. A few of the options listed will require you to use the control stick to change them and the A button to activate.

If you want to return to the cheat menu, pause the game and hold down C, Z, L, R, and joypad Left. Then move the control stick either left or right.

Codes:

Credits for Each Level: Enter your name as "(space)Credits." Choose Difficult level. When you enter the first level, you will see the end of that level and the credits.

Play as a Storm Trooper or One of Those Other Guys: Start a new game and enter your name as "(space)Wampa(two spaces)Stompa." Now get to the Battle of Hoth. When the bad guys show up, press Left on the joypad and C-Right at the same time. Then press Up on the stick. C-Right will take you through the different camera views. Check out the behind view. You're playing from the AT-ST point of view. The joypad will move the AT-ST and the Up button will activate firing. Get to the Escape from Echo Base level and press Left on the stick and the C-Right button at the same time. Then press Up on the stick. The C-Right button will switch you between Dash and the Wampa. joypad-D will move you, and the Down position will allow you to strike.

Wampa Sounds: Enter your name as ''R(space) Testers(space)ROCK.'' You'll hear Wampas when you access menu options.

GAME NAME: **STAR WARS: ROGUE SQUADRON**

ESRB RATING: **Not Rated**

THEME: **Space fighter simulation**

PLAYERS: **1**

DEVELOPED BY: **LucasArts**

PUBLISHED BY: **Nintendo**

COMMENTS: This really isn't a traditional video game, it's really a sim (simulator). All the action is in flight. You need the N64 Expansion Pack to play it. But since it was Stars Wars, I figured that you'd want to know about it. Okay, it's a great sim. Plenty of action and knock-out graphics. And, of course, all your favorite Star Wars characters. Note that it isn't the easiest game in the world to play. It takes a lot of practice to get halfway good at it.

Codes:

For a sim, this baby is loaded with codes. The way to enter them is to go to Passcodes from the initial options menu. Then you simply enter the codes.

Activate AT-ST Mini-Game: CHICKEN

Activate Imperial Gizmos and Gadgets: TOUGHGUY

Better Radar Screen: RADAR (targets above are bright while targets below are less bright)

Display End Credits: CREDITS

Filmed Sequences: DIRECTOR

Infinite Lives: IGIVEUP

Luke Makeover: Enter HARDROCK, then play through demo. Go back to Title screen and Luke has a new look.

Make the Game Harder (?!): ACE

GAME NAME: STAR FOX 64

ESRB RATING: E for Everyone. Content suitable for those 6 years or older.

THEME: Fantasy combat

PLAYERS: 1 to 4

DEVELOPED BY: Nintendo

COMMENTS: Okay, you're space mercenaries out to destroy an evil monkey Emperor called Andross on his planet Venom. Sounds like a been-there, done-that yawn, right? Wrong. This one-to four-player jet fighter video is cool because it's not just a jet fighter video. There are also battle subs and tanks. There are 15 individual missions, each one bringing you close to battling the bad-guy monkey, and each one is more difficult. Plus, there are some very cool moves and a lot of combat tough-guy radio talk from both sides. Also, when you play with multiple players, you can all fight each other. That's pretty cool, too. So, I say, if you battle only one interplanetary monkey maniac this year, make it the one in Star Fox.

Guts, glory, and the expert mode. To access the expert mode, you have to do it the old-fashioned way: Earn it. Each level/planet has a high score for enemy hits. If you can meet or beat it, then all your wingmen receive medals. So, to get to the expert mode, you have to get medals on all 15 levels without losing any wingmen. It's tough but it can be done. Following are the scores you'll need for each level of the game. Also, if you do get to the expert level, you'll have access to the sound test and graphics equalizer, which you can play around with.

Mission	Point Objective
Aquas	150
Area 6	300
Bolse	150
Corneria	150
Fotuna	50
Katina	150
Macbeth	150
Meteo	200
Mission Zones	300
Sector X	150
Sector Y	150
Sector Z	100
Solar	100
Titania	150
Venom 1	200
Venom 2	200

Tricks:

Play on Foot: To play as foot soldiers against someone in versus mode, you need to earn a medal on the planet Venom in the expert mode.

Thrills, Chills, a Moving Logo!: Use the stick to move the Star Fox insignia around on the Title screen. Not the best trick in the world, but I've seen worse.

Warping: Also, high scores in the kills department will allow you to warp to different areas on some levels. For instance, if you score 100 or more in Sector Y, you can warp to Aquas. On other areas you have to seek out the warp modes. Another good warp trick is going through all the pointy rings in Meteo. If you go through all of them, then you have enough speed to warp to Katina.

GAME NAME: **BATTLE TANX**

ESRB RATING: **T for Teen. Content suitable for those 13 years or older.**

THEME: **Military combat fighting game**

PLAYERS: **1 to 4**

DEVELOPED BY: **3DO**

COMMENTS: You drive a tank and shoot at stuff. There's some kind of story behind why you're driving around the city in tanks blowing stuff up, but who cares, right? Just hop in the tank and have a good time. You have a choice of three different tanks, including a motorcycle tank. All of them blow stuff up really well.

Codes:

All Girl Gang: Enter "WMNRSMRTR" in the Input screen to activate the Storm Ravens gang. It's an all-girl gang that features special cloaking and laser power-ups.

Gang Selection During a Campaign: To select a particular gang during a campaign, you need to enter "LTSLTSGNGS" in the Input screen.

Improved Firepower: When you collect 15 or more of a single type of weapon, press A and B at the same time. The next time you use that weapon, it will have increased firepower.

State Street (in the Windy City): Enter "CJSKPFLGMH" to play on State Street in the Chicago level. This level includes 10 lives, five Goliath tanks, and a nuclear weapon when you start game. (Note: This code is not compatible with a controller pak.)

WHERE CAN YOU GET MORE CODES AND CHEATS?

There are tons of video game magazines and books out there. New cheats and codes are discovered every day. The Internet is also a good place to learn the latest cheats, codes, and strategies. Nintendo has a very up-to-date website. So do many of the software companies, such as Acclaim and Electronic Arts. I've included the names of the publishers or developers for each game. Their sites might include some goodies about the games and maybe even some codes.

There are also a bunch of independent sites out there that offer codes. These can either be very, very good in offering the latest information and reviews or really, really bad. Once you find a good one, bookmark it.

The most important thing to remember about grabbing codes off the net is to never, ever give anyone either your home address or your e-mail address. And never accept long downloads from anyone. Anyone on the Internet who tells you a code or cheat is secret is full of it. Codes are passed on in public places, like magazines, books, and websites, for everyone to see. Think about it. You wouldn't accept a gift from a stranger on the street. You shouldn't accept codes or game programs from strangers on the Internet. And if you post a code on a site, never include your real name or e-mail address.

There is another thing you should never do on the Net, and that is accept games from anyone or any site. Never download a game from a website or accept them as gifts from someone you *met on the Net*. There are a couple of reasons for this: First, you don't know the person and you don't know who owns the website. You just shouldn't accept gifts from strangers. It's common sense. Second, you don't really know what's in the code that's going into your computer. There could be some really nasty viruses in there and you won't know it for weeks or months. Then one day you sit down to do some work, and BAMMO! GLUG, GLUG, GLUG! your entire system has crashed and the term paper you spent 3,000 hours working on has been turned to gibberish. And what are you going to tell your teacher? Space invaders ate your homework? Third, the game, if it is the actual game, has most likely been stolen. That means that the bad guys didn't steal the cart but extracted the coding for the game from the cart. It's not easy, but it can be done. And know what else? *It's against the law*.

So, play it safe and only put real Nintendo games in your system.

GET THE HOTTEST TIPS ON WINNING TODAY'S COOLEST VIDEO GAMES

HOW TO WIN AT NINTENDO 64 GAMES
Hank Schlesinger

Discover essential expert tips to help you win
at Nintendo 64.

0-312-97087-0___$5.99 U.S.___$7.99 Can.

HOW TO WIN AT SONY PLAYSTATION GAMES
Hank Schlesinger

Learn awesome expert tips to help you
ace Sony Playstation.

0-312-97100-1___$5.99 U.S.___$7.99 Can.

HOW TO BECOME A POKÉMON MASTER
Hank Schlesinger

Master the mega-popular game of monster collecting that
has spawned a cartoon series, comic books, and hundreds
of other toys.

0-312-97256-3___$5.99 U.S.___$7.99 Can.

SPORTS BOOKS THAT SCORE
FROM ST. MARTIN'S PAPERBACKS

DEREK JETER:
Pride of the Yankees, by Patrick Giles
Find out everything there is to know about the Yankees shortstop who <u>isn't</u> short on talent, looks, or heart.
0-312-97110-9___$5.99 U.S.___$7.99 Can.

MARK McGWIRE:
Home Run Hero, by Rob Rains
An in-depth look at the St. Louis Cardinal's record-breaking home-run hero.
0-312-97109-5___$5.99 U.S.___$7.99 Can.

YOU'RE OUT AND YOU'RE UGLY TOO:
Confessions of an Umpire with Attitude,
by Durwood Merrill with Jim Dent
"[A] funny and candid memoir... Here's the one ump who's not afraid to name names (both good and bad) in terms of managerial and players."   —*USA Today Baseball Weekly*
0-312-96900-7___$6.50 U.S.___$8.50 Can.

TIGER WOODS:
The Makings of a Champion, by Tim Rosaforte
A fascinating biography of one of the greatest golfers of all time—young, record-breaking Masters winner Tiger Woods.
0-312-96437-4___$5.99 U.S.___$7.99 Can.

Publishers Book and Audio Mailing Service
P.O. Box 070059, Staten Island, NY 10307
Please send me the book(s) I have checked above. I am enclosing $_____ (please add $1.50 for the first book, and $.50 for each additional book to cover postage and handling. Send check or money order only—no CODs) or charge my VISA, MASTERCARD, DISCOVER or AMERICAN EXPRESS card.

Card Number_____

Expiration date_____Signature_____

Name_____

Address_____

City_____State/Zip_____

Please allow six weeks for delivery. Prices subject to change without notice. Payment in U.S. funds only. New York residents add applicable sales tax.   SPORTA 1/99